Discover Ecuador

AVERY B. HODGES

Published by AVERY B. HODGES, 2023.

DISCOVER ECUADOR

First edition. October 6, 2023.

ISBN: 979-8223482765

Written by AVERY B. HODGES.

Table of Contents

Chapter 1: Introduction to Ecuador

Ecuador, a land of enchanting landscapes and vibrant culture, is a hidden gem nestled in the heart of South America. This diverse country offers visitors a mesmerizing blend of breathtaking natural wonders, rich history, and warm hospitality. From its awe-inspiring Andean peaks to its lush Amazon rainforests and pristine beaches, Ecuador truly has something for every traveler seeking an unforgettable adventure.

Geography:

Situated on the equator, Ecuador is bordered by Colombia to the north, Peru to the east and south, and the Pacific Ocean to the west. This small country, roughly the size of Nevada, is divided into four distinct regions: the Sierra (Andean highlands), the Oriente (Amazon rainforest), the Coast (Pacific coastline), and the Galapagos Islands. Each region boasts its own unique landscapes and ecosystems, making Ecuador a haven for nature enthusiasts and outdoor adventurers.

History:

Ecuador's history dates back thousands of years, with indigenous cultures leaving their mark on the land long before the arrival of the Spanish conquistadors. The Inca Empire once ruled over parts of present-day Ecuador, leaving behind impressive ruins such as Ingapirca and the Temple of the Sun. In 1533, the Spanish colonizers arrived, leading to centuries of colonization and the blending of European and indigenous traditions. Ecuador gained independence from Spain in 1822 and has since become a multicultural nation, celebrating its rich heritage and diversity.

Culture:

Ecuadorian culture is a vibrant tapestry woven with indigenous, Spanish, and African influences. The country's 17 indigenous groups, each with its own unique customs and languages, contribute to the rich cultural fabric of Ecuador. Traditional arts and crafts, such as weaving, pottery, and woodcarving, are still practiced by many indigenous communities, allowing visitors to witness the preservation of ancient traditions. Ecuadorians are known for their warmth and friendliness, welcoming travelers with open arms and sharing their cultural heritage through music, dance, and cuisine.

Attractions:

Ecuador offers an abundance of attractions that will captivate the hearts of travelers. Quito, the capital city, is a UNESCO World Heritage site renowned for its well-preserved colonial architecture and vibrant markets. The Galapagos Islands, a living laboratory of evolution, provide a once-in-a-lifetime opportunity to witness unique wildlife up close, including the famous giant tortoises and marine iguanas. The lush Amazon rainforest beckons adventurers with its biodiversity and indigenous communities, offering immersive experiences in nature and cultural exchange. The majestic Andean peaks, including the iconic Cotopaxi volcano, provide breathtaking vistas and thrilling outdoor activities such as hiking, climbing, and mountain biking. The coastal region invites visitors to relax on pristine beaches, explore charming fishing villages, and indulge in fresh seafood delicacies.

As you embark on your journey through Ecuador, prepare to be captivated by its natural wonders, fascinated by its history, enchanted by its culture, and embraced by its warm-hearted people. This diverse country is a true treasure trove of experiences, promising an unforgettable adventure that will leave you yearning to return time and time again.

Chapter 2: When to Visit Ecuador

Ecuador, a small country located in South America, is known for its diverse landscapes, rich culture, and remarkable biodiversity. Planning the perfect time to visit this enchanting destination is crucial to make the most out of your trip. In this chapter, we will provide you with valuable tips and insights to help you decide when to embark on your Ecuadorian adventure.

1. Climate and Weather Patterns:

Ecuador's unique geographical location near the equator grants it a varied climate throughout the year. The country can be broadly divided into four regions: the coast, the highlands, the Amazon rainforest, and the Galapagos Islands. Each region experiences distinct weather patterns, so it is essential to consider your preferred activities and destinations.

- The Coast: The coastal region of Ecuador has a tropical climate, with temperatures ranging from 23°C to 32°C (73°F to 89°F). The dry season, from June to December, is ideal for beach activities and water sports.

- The Highlands: Ecuador's highlands, including the capital city of Quito, boast a mild climate due to their elevation. Temperatures range from 7°C to 24°C (45°F to 75°F) during the day, with cooler nights. The dry season, from June to September, is the best time to explore the Andean landscapes and indigenous markets.

- The Amazon Rainforest: The Amazon region experiences a tropical rainforest climate, with high humidity and rainfall year-round. However, the driest months are from November to February, making it easier to navigate the dense jungle and spot wildlife.

- The Galapagos Islands: The Galapagos Islands have a unique climate, influenced by ocean currents. The warm season, from December to May, offers pleasant temperatures and clear waters for snorkeling and diving. The dry season, from June to November, brings cooler temperatures and a chance to witness unique wildlife, such as penguins and sea lions.

2. Festivals and Cultural Events:

If you wish to immerse yourself in Ecuador's vibrant culture and traditions, planning your visit around festivals can be a fantastic idea. The country celebrates numerous festivals throughout the year, showcasing its rich heritage and religious customs. Some notable events include:

- Inti Raymi: Celebrated on June 24th, this Incan festival marks the winter solstice and honors the sun god Inti. The most prominent celebrations take place in the city of Cuenca, where locals dress in traditional attire and participate in colorful parades.

- Fiesta de la Mama Negra: Held in Latacunga during the second week of September, this festival combines indigenous, mestizo, and Spanish traditions. It pays homage to the Virgen de la Merced and features vibrant processions, music, and dancing.

- Carnival: Ecuador's Carnival takes place in February or March, depending on the year. This lively celebration involves water fights, parades, and the famous mud battles in the town of Guaranda.

3. Wildlife Viewing Opportunities:

Ecuador is a haven for nature enthusiasts, offering unparalleled opportunities to witness unique wildlife species. To make the most of your wildlife encounters, consider the following:

- The Galapagos Islands: As a UNESCO World Heritage site, the Galapagos Islands are renowned for their incredible biodiversity and endemic species. Depending on your interests, you can plan your visit to coincide with the breeding seasons of various animals, such as sea turtles, marine iguanas, or blue-footed boobies.

- The Amazon Rainforest: While wildlife can be observed year-round in the Amazon, the dry season offers better chances of spotting elusive creatures due to reduced foliage. Keep in mind that heavy rains may limit accessibility to certain areas during the wetter months.

By considering the climate, festivals, and wildlife viewing opportunities, you can determine the best time to visit Ecuador based on your preferences. Remember to pack accordingly, and always check for any travel advisories or restrictions before your journey. Ecuador welcomes you with open arms, ready to provide an unforgettable experience filled with natural wonders and cultural treasures.

Chapter 3: What to Pack for Your Trip to Ecuador

Introduction:

Preparing for your trip to Ecuador can be an exciting and overwhelming experience, especially when it comes to deciding what to pack. Ecuador's diverse landscapes, from the Amazon rainforest to the Andes Mountains and the Galapagos Islands, offer a wide range of activities and climates. In this chapter, we will guide you on what essentials to pack to ensure a comfortable and enjoyable journey through this beautiful country.

1. Clothing:

Ecuador's climate varies greatly depending on the region you plan to visit. It is advisable to pack clothes suitable for both warm and cool weather. Here are some essentials to consider:

a) Lightweight clothing: Pack breathable and quick-drying clothes such as cotton or linen shirts, shorts, and skirts for the coastal areas and the Amazon rainforest.

b) Layering options: As temperatures can drop significantly in the highlands, especially during the evenings, it is essential to bring a few warm layers such as sweaters, jackets, and long pants.

c) Rain gear: Ecuador's weather can be unpredictable, so it's always wise to pack a lightweight rain jacket or poncho to stay dry during unexpected showers.

d) Comfortable footwear: Whether you plan to hike in the Andes or explore the cobblestone streets of Quito, comfortable walking shoes or hiking boots are a must.

2. Outdoor Essentials:

Ecuador's breathtaking landscapes offer numerous opportunities for outdoor adventures. To make the most of your trip, be sure to pack the following items:

a) Daypack: A small backpack is essential for day trips and hikes, allowing you to carry water, snacks, sunscreen, insect repellent, and other necessities.

b) Hat and sunglasses: Ecuador's proximity to the equator means stronger sun rays. Protect yourself from the sun by packing a wide-brimmed hat and UV-blocking sunglasses.

c) Swimsuit: Don't forget to pack a swimsuit, as you might want to take a dip in the Pacific Ocean or enjoy the thermal baths in Baños.

d) Binoculars: If you plan to visit the Galapagos Islands or explore Ecuador's rich birdlife, a pair of binoculars will enhance your wildlife viewing experience.

3. Health and Safety:

Taking care of your health and safety while traveling is crucial. Here are a few items to include in your packing list:

a) Medications: If you have any pre-existing medical conditions or require specific medications, ensure you have an ample supply for the duration of your trip.

b) Insect repellent: Protect yourself against mosquitoes and other insects by packing a reliable insect repellent containing DEET.

c) First aid kit: It's always wise to carry a basic first aid kit with essentials such as band-aids, antiseptic cream, and any personal medication.

d) Travel insurance: Before embarking on your journey, make sure you have comprehensive travel insurance that covers medical emergencies, trip cancellations, and lost belongings.

Conclusion:

Packing for your trip to Ecuador requires careful consideration of the diverse climates and activities you plan to undertake. By packing the essentials mentioned in this chapter, you will be well-prepared to explore Ecuador's stunning landscapes, immerse yourself in its vibrant culture, and make unforgettable memories. Remember to pack light, stay comfortable, and embrace the adventure that awaits you in Ecuador!

Chapter 4: Geography and Climate of Ecuador

Introduction:

Welcome to Chapter 4 of our tourist guide on Ecuador! In this chapter, we will explore the fascinating geography and climate of this beautiful country. From towering mountains to winding rivers, serene lakes, and stunning coastlines, Ecuador offers a diverse range of landscapes that will leave you in awe. Additionally, we will discuss the climate and what you can expect during your visit. So, let's embark on this geographical and climatic journey through Ecuador!

1. Mountains:

Ecuador is renowned for its breathtaking mountain ranges, which are part of the Andes, the world's longest continental mountain range. The country is home to numerous majestic peaks, including the iconic Cotopaxi, Chimborazo, and Cayambe. These mountains not only offer awe-inspiring views but also provide excellent opportunities for hiking, climbing, and adventure sports. As you ascend, be prepared for changing temperatures and breathtaking vistas that will take your breath away.

2. Rivers and Lakes:

Ecuador boasts an extensive network of rivers and lakes, which play a crucial role in shaping its geography and providing habitats for diverse flora and fauna. The mighty Amazon River, originating in the Andes, flows through Ecuadorian territory, offering opportunities for river exploration and wildlife encounters. Additionally, the country is dotted with enchanting lakes such as Quilotoa, Cuicocha, and San Pablo, each with its unique charm and surrounded by stunning landscapes. These natural wonders are perfect for boating, fishing, or simply immersing yourself in the tranquility of nature.

3. Coastline:

Ecuador's coastline stretches along the Pacific Ocean, offering a contrasting landscape to its mountainous regions. The coastal region is characterized by long stretches of sandy beaches, vibrant fishing villages, and a rich marine ecosystem. Here, you can indulge in water sports like surfing, diving, and snorkeling, or simply relax under the warm sun while enjoying fresh seafood delicacies. Don't forget to explore the captivating Galapagos Islands, a UNESCO World Heritage Site, which are part of Ecuador's territory and home to unique wildlife.

4. Climate:

Ecuador's climate is as diverse as its geography, thanks to its location on the equator. The country experiences four distinct regions: the Amazon Rainforest, the Andean highlands, the coastal lowlands, and the Galapagos Islands. The climate varies significantly depending on the altitude and proximity to the ocean. In the highlands, including cities like Quito and Cuenca, expect a mild and spring-like climate year-round, with cooler temperatures at higher elevations. The coastal region enjoys a tropical climate, with warm temperatures and high humidity. The Amazon Rainforest experiences a hot and humid climate, while the Galapagos Islands have a unique subtropical climate with mild temperatures and distinct wet and dry seasons.

Conclusion:

As you can see, Ecuador's geography and climate offer a diverse range of experiences for every traveler. From the awe-inspiring mountains to the enchanting rivers, lakes, and captivating coastline, this country is a true paradise for nature enthusiasts. Whether you seek adventure, relaxation, or wildlife encounters, Ecuador has it all. So, pack your bags and get ready to explore the remarkable landscapes and experience the diverse climates that make Ecuador a truly unique destination.

Chapter 5: The Regions of Ecuador

Introduction:

Ecuador, a small country located on the equator in South America, is known for its incredible diversity in landscapes and ecosystems. This chapter will delve into the different regions of Ecuador and highlight their unique characteristics, offering travelers a glimpse into the natural wonders that await them.

1. The Andean Highlands:

The Andean Highlands occupy the central part of Ecuador and are home to majestic snow-capped mountains, picturesque valleys, and traditional indigenous communities. This region is famous for its vibrant markets, where visitors can immerse themselves in the rich culture and purchase handmade crafts. Hiking enthusiasts can explore the stunning Cotopaxi National Park, which houses one of the world's highest active volcanoes, while nature lovers can marvel at the breathtaking Quilotoa crater lake.

2. The Amazon Rainforest:

Covering a significant portion of Ecuador's eastern region, the Amazon Rainforest is a true paradise for nature enthusiasts. This biodiverse region is teeming with exotic wildlife, including jaguars, monkeys, and vibrant bird species. Visitors can embark on guided tours through the dense jungle, learning about the indigenous communities that call this region home and discovering the secrets of traditional medicinal plants. Experiencing an overnight stay in an eco-lodge deep within the rainforest is an unforgettable adventure.

3. The Pacific Coast:

Ecuador's Pacific Coast stretches along the western edge of the country, offering visitors stunning beaches, vibrant coastal cities, and an abundance of marine life. The region is famous for its surf spots, attracting wave enthusiasts from around the world. In addition to the thrill of catching the perfect wave, visitors can also witness the annual migration of humpback whales, which come to breed in the warm waters off the coast. The coastal towns of Montañita and Puerto Lopez are popular destinations, offering a lively atmosphere and delicious seafood cuisine.

4. The Galapagos Islands:

No visit to Ecuador would be complete without exploring the unique Galapagos Islands. Located approximately 1,000 kilometers off the mainland, this archipelago is renowned for its unparalleled biodiversity and played a significant role in Charles Darwin's theory of evolution. Visitors can encounter iconic species such as giant tortoises, marine iguanas, and blue-footed boobies. Snorkeling and diving opportunities abound, allowing travelers to immerse themselves in the underwater wonders of this UNESCO World Heritage site.

Conclusion:

Ecuador's diverse regions offer a plethora of experiences for every type of traveler. From the awe-inspiring Andean Highlands to the enchanting Amazon Rainforest, the stunning Pacific Coast to the captivating Galapagos Islands, this country truly has it all. By exploring these unique regions, visitors will gain a deeper understanding of Ecuador's rich natural heritage and cultural diversity, creating memories that will last a lifetime.

Chapter 6: History and Culture of Ecuador

Introduction:

Ecuador, a land of diverse landscapes and vibrant cultures, boasts a rich history that has shaped its present-day identity. From the ancient indigenous civilizations to the Spanish conquest and subsequent struggles for independence, this chapter delves into the captivating history and unique culture of Ecuador.

1. The Early Inhabitants:

The history of Ecuador dates back thousands of years, with evidence of human presence as early as 10,000 BCE. The region was home to various indigenous groups, including the Quitu, Cañari, and Inca civilizations. These ancient cultures left behind impressive architectural wonders, such as the Ingapirca ruins, which stand as a testament to their advanced engineering and agricultural practices.

2. The Arrival of the Spanish:

In 1533, the Spanish conquistador Francisco Pizarro arrived in Ecuador, marking the beginning of Spanish colonial rule. The indigenous populations suffered greatly under Spanish oppression, forced labor, and the introduction of diseases. This era saw the blending of indigenous and Spanish cultures, giving rise to a unique mestizo identity that remains prominent in Ecuadorian society today.

3. Independence and the Birth of a Nation:

Inspired by the ideals of the French and American revolutions, Ecuador, along with other South American countries, fought for independence from Spain in the early 19th century. On May 24, 1822, the Battle of Pichincha marked a decisive victory for the forces led by the liberator Simón Bolívar, leading to Ecuador's independence from Spanish rule. The nation was named Ecuador due to its location on the equator, symbolizing its geographic significance.

4. Political Turmoil and Modernization:

Ecuador's post-independence history has been marked by political instability, with numerous changes in government and struggles for power. The discovery of oil reserves in the mid-20th century brought both economic prosperity and political challenges. The exploitation of these resources resulted in environmental concerns, leading to a growing awareness of the importance of sustainable development and the preservation of Ecuador's unique ecosystems.

5. Cultural Diversity and Traditions:

Ecuador is renowned for its cultural diversity, with over 14 indigenous nationalities and a rich mestizo heritage. Each region of the country boasts its own distinct traditions, music, dance, and cuisine. Visitors can immerse themselves in the vibrant festivals, such as the Inti Raymi, where ancient rituals are celebrated, or the colorful Otavalo Market, which showcases traditional crafts and textiles.

6. Historical Figures and Sites:

Throughout Ecuador's history, several notable figures have emerged, leaving a lasting impact on the country's culture and identity. Francisco de Orellana, the Spanish explorer, embarked on a legendary expedition down the Amazon River, contributing to the exploration and mapping of the region. Additionally, the legacy of revolutionary figures such as Simón Bolívar and Eloy Alfaro remains significant in Ecuadorian history.

Conclusion:

Ecuador's history and culture are intertwined, forming a captivating tapestry that reflects the resilience and diversity of its people. From ancient civilizations to colonial rule and struggles for independence, this chapter has provided a glimpse into the vibrant past that has shaped Ecuador into the enchanting destination it is today. As you explore this remarkable country, take time to appreciate its historical sites, engage with its cultural traditions, and embrace the warmth and hospitality of its people.

Chapter 7: Language and People of Ecuador

Introduction:

In this chapter, we will explore the fascinating world of language and people in Ecuador. Ecuador is a diverse country, both in terms of its landscapes and its people. With a rich cultural heritage and a wide range of languages spoken, understanding the language and customs of Ecuador is essential for any traveler wishing to immerse themselves in the local culture. This chapter will provide a brief overview of the languages spoken in Ecuador, some common phrases, language tips for travelers, and insights into social customs and etiquette.

Languages Spoken in Ecuador:

Ecuador is a multilingual country, with Spanish being the official language. However, there are also several indigenous languages spoken by various ethnic groups. Some of the most prominent indigenous languages include Quechua, Shuar, and Kichwa. While Spanish is widely spoken throughout the country, especially in urban areas, knowing a few basic phrases in these indigenous languages can greatly enhance your experience and interactions with the local communities.

Common Phrases:

To help you navigate your way through Ecuador, here are some common phrases in Spanish that will prove useful during your travels:

1. Greetings:

- ¡Hola! - Hello!
- Buenos días - Good morning!
- Buenas tardes - Good afternoon!
- Buenas noches - Good evening/night!

2. Basic Phrases:

- Por favor - Please
- Gracias - Thank you

- ¿Cómo estás? - How are you?
- ¿Cuánto cuesta? - How much does it cost?
- ¿Dónde está...? - Where is...?

Language Tips for Travelers:

While Spanish is the dominant language in Ecuador, it is essential to note that there are some regional variations in vocabulary and pronunciation. Here are a few language tips to help you communicate effectively:

1. Learn some basic Spanish phrases before your trip.
2. Practice your pronunciation to be better understood by locals.
3. Carry a pocket-sized Spanish-English dictionary or use translation apps.
4. Engage in language exchange opportunities with locals to improve your skills.
5. Be patient and open-minded when communicating with people who have limited English proficiency.

Social Customs and Etiquette:

Understanding the social customs and etiquette in Ecuador will ensure that you have a respectful and enjoyable experience. Here are a few key points to keep in mind:

1. Greetings: Shake hands and make eye contact when meeting someone for the first time. Kissing on the cheek is common among friends and family.
2. Personal Space: Ecuadorians tend to stand closer during conversations than in some other cultures. Respect personal space but be prepared for a closer proximity.
3. Time: Punctuality is appreciated, but it is not uncommon for events or meetings to start a little late. However, it is best to arrive on time to show respect for the host.
4. Dining Etiquette: When invited to someone's home, it is customary to bring a small gift. It is polite to try a little of everything served and to compliment the host's cooking.

5. Respect for Indigenous Cultures: When visiting indigenous communities, it is important to respect their customs, traditions, and beliefs. Seek permission before taking photographs and follow any guidelines provided by the community.

Conclusion:

Language and people are integral aspects of Ecuador's cultural tapestry. By familiarizing yourself with the languages spoken, learning some common phrases, and understanding the social customs and etiquette, you will be able to connect with the people of Ecuador on a deeper level. Embrace the diversity and richness of Ecuador's language and people, and you will undoubtedly have an unforgettable experience in this beautiful country.

Chapter 8: Traditional Cuisine of Ecuador

Introduction:

Ecuador, a country known for its rich biodiversity and stunning landscapes, also boasts a diverse and flavorful culinary tradition. In this chapter, we will delve into the traditional cuisine of Ecuador, exploring its most popular dishes, unique ingredients, and where to find the best food in the country. Additionally, we will provide cooking tips and recipes for those eager to recreate these delicious flavors in their own kitchens.

1. A Taste of Ecuador:

Ecuadorian cuisine is a reflection of the country's geographical diversity, with each region offering its own distinct flavors and specialties. From the coastal regions with their abundance of seafood to the highlands with hearty stews and soups, there is something to satisfy every palate.

2. Popular Ecuadorian Dishes:

a. Ceviche: A beloved coastal dish, ceviche is made with fresh seafood marinated in citrus juices, onions, and herbs. It is often served with plantain chips or toasted corn.

b. Llapingachos: A staple of Ecuadorian cuisine, llapingachos are potato pancakes stuffed with cheese and served with a peanut sauce. They are commonly enjoyed as a side dish or as part of a traditional breakfast.

c. Seco de Pollo: This flavorful chicken stew is made with a base of onions, garlic, tomatoes, and spices. It is typically served with rice, avocado, and a side of crunchy fried plantains.

d. Fanesca: A traditional soup commonly enjoyed during Easter, fanesca is a hearty blend of grains, legumes, and vegetables, including pumpkin, corn, and beans. It is often topped with hard-boiled eggs and served with empanadas.

3. Unique Ingredients:

Ecuadorian cuisine incorporates a variety of unique ingredients that contribute to its distinct flavors. Some notable ingredients include:

a. Achiote: Also known as annatto, achiote is a spice derived from the seeds of the annatto tree. It adds a vibrant red color and a subtle earthy flavor to dishes.

b. Choclo: A type of Andean corn, choclo has large, tender kernels that are often used in soups, stews, and ceviche.

c. Mote: Mote refers to hominy, which is corn kernels that have been soaked and cooked until they become soft and chewy. It is commonly used in soups and stews.

4. Where to Find the Best Food:

Ecuador offers a plethora of culinary delights, and certain cities and regions are renowned for their exceptional food. Some must-visit destinations for food enthusiasts include:

a. Quito: The capital city boasts a vibrant food scene, with traditional markets, street food stalls, and upscale restaurants offering a wide range of Ecuadorian dishes.

b. Guayaquil: Located on the coast, Guayaquil is a seafood lover's paradise. The Malecón 2000 boardwalk is a popular spot to indulge in fresh ceviche and other coastal delicacies.

c. Cuenca: Known for its high-quality ingredients and traditional recipes, Cuenca offers a taste of authentic Ecuadorian cuisine. Don't miss the famous Cuy Asado a roasted guinea pig dish.

5. Cooking Tips and Recipes:

For those eager to recreate Ecuadorian flavors at home, here are a few cooking tips and recipes:

a. Use fresh and locally sourced ingredients whenever possible to enhance the authenticity of the dishes.

b. Experiment with traditional Ecuadorian spices and herbs, such as achiote, cilantro, and cumin, to add depth of flavor to your recipes.

c. Try your hand at making classic Ecuadorian dishes like ceviche, llapingachos, or fanesca using traditional recipes. Don't be afraid to put your own twist on them!

Conclusion:

Ecuadorian cuisine is a true reflection of the country's culture and diversity. From the coastal regions to the highlands, each dish tells a story and offers a unique culinary experience. Whether you're exploring the bustling markets of Quito or enjoying a seafood feast in Guayaquil, the traditional cuisine of Ecuador is sure to leave a lasting impression on your taste buds.

Chapter 9: Modern Cuisine of Ecuador

Introduction:

Ecuador, a country known for its diverse culture and stunning landscapes, is also gaining recognition for its modern cuisine. This chapter will provide an overview of the contemporary culinary scene in Ecuador, highlighting its most popular dishes and ingredients. Additionally, we will explore where to find the best food in the country, along with cooking tips and authentic recipes that will allow you to recreate the flavors of Ecuador in your own kitchen.

1. Fusion of Traditions:

Ecuadorian modern cuisine is a delightful fusion of traditional flavors and innovative techniques. Drawing inspiration from indigenous ingredients and international influences, chefs in Ecuador have created a unique culinary identity that showcases the country's rich gastronomic heritage. From the coastal regions to the Andean highlands and the Amazon rainforest, each area contributes its own distinct flavors and ingredients to the modern cuisine of Ecuador.

2. Popular Dishes:

a) Ceviche de Camarón: A refreshing coastal dish made with shrimp marinated in lime juice, red onions, tomatoes, and cilantro. This zesty appetizer perfectly captures the essence of Ecuador's coastal cuisine.

b) Locro de Papa: A hearty potato and cheese soup that originated in the Andean highlands. This comforting dish is made with potatoes, cheese, onions, garlic, and various herbs, creating a flavorful and satisfying meal.

c) Seco de Chivo: A succulent goat stew cooked with beer, cilantro, and spices. This traditional dish from the Sierra region showcases the use of local ingredients and slow-cooking methods, resulting in tender and flavorful meat.

3. Key Ingredients:

a) Quinoa: A nutritious grain that has been a staple in the Andean diet for centuries. Quinoa is often used as a base for salads, soups, and main dishes, providing a healthy and protein-rich alternative to rice or pasta.

b) Plantains: A versatile fruit that is a common ingredient in Ecuadorian cuisine. Plantains can be boiled, fried, or mashed, and are used in various dishes, including bolones (mashed plantain balls) and patacones (fried plantain slices).

c) Amazonian Fruits: Ecuador's Amazon rainforest is home to a vast array of exotic fruits, such as the maracuyá (passion fruit), guanábana (soursop), and chirimoya (custard apple). These fruits are often used in desserts, juices, and cocktails, adding a tropical twist to Ecuadorian cuisine.

4. Where to Find the Best Food:

To experience the best of Ecuadorian modern cuisine, consider visiting the vibrant cities of Quito and Guayaquil. These urban hubs offer a wide range of restaurants and food markets, where you can sample both traditional and contemporary dishes. Additionally, exploring local food festivals and seeking recommendations from locals will lead you to hidden culinary gems throughout the country.

5. Cooking Tips and Recipes:

To truly immerse yourself in Ecuadorian cuisine, try your hand at preparing some authentic dishes. Here are two recipes to get you started:

a) Recipe: Ceviche de Camarón

Ingredients:

- 1 pound of fresh shrimp, peeled and deveined
- 4 limes, juiced
- 1 red onion, thinly sliced
- 2 tomatoes, diced
- Handful of fresh cilantro, chopped
- Salt and pepper to taste

Instructions:

1. In a bowl, combine the shrimp and lime juice. Let it marinate for 15 minutes, allowing the lime juice to cook the shrimp.

2. Add the red onion, tomatoes, and cilantro to the bowl. Season with salt and pepper, and mix well.

3. Serve the ceviche chilled, either as an appetizer or a light meal. Enjoy the vibrant flavors of Ecuador's coastal cuisine!

b) Recipe: Locro de Papa

Ingredients:

- 4 large potatoes, peeled and diced
- 1 white onion, finely chopped
- 2 cloves of garlic, minced
- 2 cups of milk
- 1 cup of cheese (queso fresco or mozzarella), grated
- Handful of fresh cilantro, chopped
- Salt and pepper to taste

Instructions:

1. In a large pot, boil the potatoes until tender. Drain and set aside.

2. In a separate pan, sauté the onion and garlic until golden brown.

3. Add the cooked potatoes to the pan, along with the milk. Mash the potatoes slightly to thicken the soup.

4. Stir in the grated cheese, cilantro, salt, and pepper. Cook for an additional 5 minutes, until the cheese melts and the flavors combine.

5. Serve the locro de papa hot, garnished with extra cilantro. Enjoy the comforting flavors of Ecuador's Andean cuisine!

Conclusion:

Ecuador's modern cuisine offers a delightful blend of traditional flavors and contemporary culinary techniques. From the coastal ceviche to the hearty Andean soups, each dish tells a story of Ecuador's diverse culinary heritage. By exploring the country's best food establishments, experimenting with authentic recipes, and embracing the use of local ingredients, you can embark on a gastronomic journey that will leave your taste buds craving for more.

Chapter 10: Drinks and Beverages of Ecuador

Introduction:

Ecuador, a country known for its rich biodiversity and stunning landscapes, is also home to a diverse range of drinks and beverages that reflect its cultural heritage. In this chapter, we will explore the unique and flavorful world of Ecuadorian drinks, including both alcoholic and non-alcoholic options. From traditional favorites to hidden gems, we will guide you to the best places to indulge in Ecuador's vibrant beverage scene.

1. Traditional Alcoholic Beverages:

1.1 Chicha: Chicha is a traditional fermented corn or yuca beverage that has been enjoyed in Ecuador for centuries. It is often consumed during festivals and special occasions, and its unique taste and texture make it a must-try for adventurous travelers. You can find chicha in local markets or traditional restaurants, where it is often served in large clay pots.

1.2 Canelazo: This warm and comforting drink is particularly popular in the Andean region of Ecuador, especially during the colder months. Made with aguardiente (a type of sugar cane liquor), cinnamon, and naranjilla juice, canelazo is the perfect beverage to warm you up after a long day of exploring the stunning highlands.

1.3 Pilsener: Ecuador's most famous beer, Pilsener, is a crisp and refreshing lager that is widely consumed throughout the country. Whether you're enjoying a beach day or exploring the bustling streets of Quito, you'll find Pilsener readily available in bars, restaurants, and convenience stores.

2. Non-Alcoholic Beverages:

2.1 Morocho: A popular street food drink, morocho is a thick and creamy beverage made from purple corn, milk, cinnamon, and sugar.

Often served hot, it is a comforting and delicious treat that can be found in local markets or street stalls.

2.2 Horchata: Horchata is a refreshing non-alcoholic beverage made from ground rice, cinnamon, and sugar. It is commonly enjoyed as a cool and creamy drink, especially during the hot summer months. Look for it in cafes or juice bars, where it is often served over ice.

2.3 Guayusa: Known as Ecuador's superleaf guayusa is a herbal tea made from the leaves of the Ilex guayusa tree. It is known for its energizing properties and is often consumed in the morning to kickstart the day. You can find guayusa in local markets or specialty tea shops, where it is often served hot or cold.

3. Where to Find the Best Drinks:

3.1 Quito: The capital city offers a wide range of bars, restaurants, and cafes where you can sample both traditional and modern Ecuadorian beverages. Head to the historic Old Town for a taste of traditional chicha or explore the trendy La Mariscal neighborhood for a vibrant nightlife scene.

3.2 Guayaquil: Ecuador's largest city is known for its bustling markets and vibrant street food culture. Visit the Malecon 2000, a waterfront promenade, to find a variety of stalls and vendors selling traditional drinks like morocho and canelazo.

3.3 Otavalo: This charming town in the Andean highlands is famous for its indigenous market, where you can find an array of traditional beverages. Don't miss the opportunity to try fresh fruit juices and herbal teas made from locally grown ingredients.

Conclusion:

Ecuador's drinks and beverages offer a delightful glimpse into the country's cultural heritage and natural abundance. From traditional favorites like chicha and canelazo to refreshing non-alcoholic options like morocho and guayusa tea, there is something to satisfy every palate. Whether you're exploring the bustling cities or immersing yourself in the stunning landscapes, be sure to indulge in Ecuador's vibrant beverage scene for a truly authentic experience.

Chapter 11: Dining out in Ecuador

Introduction:

Ecuador is a country known for its rich culinary traditions and diverse gastronomy. From the coastal regions to the highlands and the Amazon rainforest, Ecuador offers a plethora of dining options that will satisfy even the most discerning palate. In this chapter, we will provide you with valuable tips on how to choose a restaurant, order food, and pay the bill. Additionally, we will recommend some exceptional dining establishments in different parts of the country to enhance your culinary experience in Ecuador.

Choosing a Restaurant:

When it comes to selecting a restaurant in Ecuador, there are a few factors to consider. First and foremost, it is essential to prioritize hygiene and cleanliness. Look for restaurants with good ratings and reviews, or those that display a Certificado de Calidad (Quality Certificate) issued by the Ministry of Tourism. These certificates ensure that the establishment meets certain standards of hygiene and food safety.

Another crucial aspect to consider is the restaurant's specialization. Ecuadorian cuisine is incredibly diverse, so it's worth exploring different regional dishes. Whether you're in the coastal region and craving ceviche, or in the highlands yearning for a hearty bowl of locro de papa, choose a restaurant that specializes in the local cuisine you wish to try.

Ordering Food:

Once you've chosen a restaurant, it's time to dive into the menu. Ecuadorian menus typically offer a variety of options, from traditional dishes to international cuisine. To fully immerse yourself in the local culinary scene, we recommend trying traditional Ecuadorian dishes like llapingachos (potato patties), seco de chivo (goat stew), or encebollado (fish soup).

If you have dietary restrictions or allergies, don't hesitate to inform your server. Ecuadorian restaurants are generally accommodating and can often provide alternatives or make adjustments to suit your needs. Additionally, it's worth noting that portion sizes in Ecuador are usually generous, so consider sharing dishes or asking for a half portion if you have a smaller appetite.

Paying the Bill:

When it comes time to settle the bill, it's customary to ask for the cuenta (bill) from your server. In Ecuador, tipping is not mandatory, but it is appreciated. A 10% tip is considered generous, but feel free to adjust the amount based on the quality of service you received.

It's important to note that some restaurants in Ecuador may only accept cash, especially in more remote areas. Therefore, it's advisable to carry some local currency with you. However, in larger cities and tourist areas, credit cards are widely accepted.

Recommended Restaurants:

1. Guayaquil - La Canoa: Located in the heart of Guayaquil, La Canoa offers a delightful fusion of Ecuadorian and international cuisine. With its charming ambiance and exquisite dishes, this restaurant is a must-visit for food enthusiasts.

2. Quito - Zazu: Situated in Quito's historic center, Zazu is renowned for its innovative take on Ecuadorian cuisine. The restaurant's commitment to using locally sourced ingredients and its unique flavor combinations make it a top choice for culinary adventurers.

3. Cuenca - Raymipampa: A popular spot among locals and tourists alike, Raymipampa offers a wide range of traditional Ecuadorian dishes. From roasted cuy (guinea pig) to hearty soups, this restaurant provides an authentic taste of Cuenca's gastronomy.

Conclusion:

Dining out in Ecuador is an experience that should not be missed. By following these tips on choosing a restaurant, ordering food, and paying the bill, you can ensure a seamless and enjoyable dining experience. The recommended restaurants mentioned in this chapter will further elevate your journey through Ecuador's vibrant culinary landscape. Bon appétit!

Chapter 12: Food and Drink Festivals in Ecuador

Ecuador, a country known for its rich culinary heritage and diverse gastronomy, hosts a plethora of vibrant food and drink festivals throughout the year. These festivals provide an excellent opportunity for both locals and tourists to indulge in traditional Ecuadorian cuisine, sample exotic flavors, and immerse themselves in the country's vibrant cultural traditions. In this chapter, we will explore some of the most prominent food and drink festivals that take place in Ecuador, offering a unique and unforgettable experience for all gastronomy enthusiasts.

1. Festival de la Fruta y de las Flores (Fruit and Flower Festival) - Ambato:

Kicking off the festival calendar in Ecuador is the renowned Festival de la Fruta y de las Flores, held annually in Ambato during the month of February. This colorful event showcases the country's diverse agricultural produce, including an array of tropical fruits and vibrant flowers. Visitors can enjoy delicious fruit-based dishes, freshly squeezed juices, and traditional Ecuadorian desserts, all while marveling at the stunning floral displays and participating in lively parades.

2. Festival de la Cerveza (Beer Festival) - Quito:

Beer aficionados should mark their calendars for the Festival de la Cerveza, held in Quito during the month of April. This festival celebrates Ecuador's emerging craft beer scene, bringing together local and international breweries to showcase their finest brews. Visitors can savor a wide range of beer styles, from traditional Ecuadorian chicha to innovative craft creations, while enjoying live music, beer tasting competitions, and gastronomic delights that perfectly complement the refreshing beverages.

3. Festival del Cuy (Guinea Pig Festival) - Cuenca:

In the charming city of Cuenca, the Festival del Cuy takes place in June, paying homage to one of Ecuador's most iconic delicacies – guinea pig. This festival offers a unique opportunity to taste traditional dishes featuring cuy as the main ingredient, prepared in various mouthwatering ways. Visitors can also witness guinea pig competitions, learn about the cultural significance of this dish, and immerse themselves in the local customs and traditions surrounding its consumption.

4. Festival del Chocolate (Chocolate Festival) - Quito and Guayaquil:

For chocolate lovers, the Festival del Chocolate is a must-visit event held in both Quito and Guayaquil during the month of August. Ecuador is renowned for its high-quality cacao, and this festival celebrates the country's rich chocolate heritage. Visitors can indulge in a wide variety of chocolate-based treats, attend workshops to learn about the bean-to-bar process, and witness chocolate-making demonstrations by expert chocolatiers. This festival offers a true sensory experience, with the opportunity to taste and appreciate Ecuador's finest chocolates.

5. Festival de la Gastronomía (Gastronomy Festival) - Loja:

Wrapping up the year in November is the Festival de la Gastronomía, held in the city of Loja. This festival celebrates the diverse culinary traditions of Ecuador, showcasing regional specialties from different provinces across the country. Visitors can sample a wide range of dishes, from hearty mountain stews to coastal seafood delicacies, all while enjoying live music, traditional dance performances, and cultural exhibitions that highlight the unique heritage of each region.

These are just a few examples of the many food and drink festivals that Ecuador has to offer throughout the year. Each festival provides an opportunity to immerse oneself in the country's rich culinary traditions, taste unique flavors, and engage with the vibrant culture of Ecuador. Whether you are a food enthusiast or simply looking to explore Ecuador's cultural heritage, attending these festivals is sure to be an unforgettable experience.

Chapter 13: Getting to Ecuador

Introduction:

Ecuador, a country located in the northwestern part of South America, is a land of stunning natural landscapes, vibrant culture, and rich biodiversity. To experience the wonders of this country, it is essential to know the various modes of transportation available for travelers. This chapter will provide you with detailed information on how to reach Ecuador, including by plane, train, bus, car, and ferry. Whether you prefer convenience, adventure, or a mix of both, there is a transportation option suitable for every traveler.

1. By Plane:

Flying to Ecuador is the most common and convenient way to reach the country. The Mariscal Sucre International Airport, located near Quito, is the major gateway for international travelers. Several airlines offer direct flights to Ecuador from major cities worldwide. For those looking to explore the Galapagos Islands, there are flights available from Quito or Guayaquil to Baltra or San Cristobal airports.

2. By Train:

Although Ecuador's train network is not extensive, it offers a unique and scenic way to travel through the country. The famous Tren Crucero, a luxury train journey, takes you on a captivating route from Quito to Guayaquil, passing through breathtaking landscapes, indigenous villages, and historic sites. This train ride is a perfect choice for those seeking a memorable and leisurely travel experience.

3. By Bus:

Traveling by bus is a cost-effective and popular option for getting around Ecuador. The country has a well-developed bus network that connects major cities and towns. From neighboring countries like Colombia and Peru, international bus services are available, providing a convenient way to enter Ecuador. It is advisable to choose reputable bus companies with comfortable and reliable services.

4. By Car:

For travelers who prefer flexibility and independence, renting a car is an excellent option to explore Ecuador. The country has a good road infrastructure, allowing you to navigate through diverse landscapes at your own pace. However, it is essential to be aware of local traffic regulations and road conditions. Renting a car gives you the freedom to discover hidden gems and off-the-beaten-path destinations.

5. By Ferry:

If you are an adventurous traveler or wish to explore Ecuador's coastal regions, taking a ferry can be an exciting option. Ferries operate between mainland Ecuador and the Galapagos Islands, providing an unforgettable journey across the Pacific Ocean. This mode of transportation offers stunning views of the ocean and the opportunity to spot marine wildlife along the way.

Conclusion:

Getting to Ecuador is an adventure in itself, with a range of transportation options to suit every traveler's preferences. Whether you choose to fly for convenience, take a train for a unique experience, hop on a bus for affordability, drive for flexibility, or embark on a ferry for an exciting journey, each mode of transportation offers its own charm. Plan your trip wisely, considering your budget, time constraints, and desired level of adventure, and get ready to explore the wonders of Ecuador.

Chapter 14: Getting Around by Public Transportation in Ecuador

Introduction:

Ecuador, a country known for its diverse landscapes and rich cultural heritage, offers a wide range of public transportation options for travelers to explore its beauty. From the bustling capital city of Quito to the charming towns nestled in the Andes Mountains, this chapter will guide you through the different types of public transportation available in Ecuador, including trains, buses, and metros. Additionally, we will provide you with a helpful map of the public transportation system in Quito, the capital city, to ensure a smooth and convenient journey.

1. Trains:

Ecuador boasts a remarkable train network that allows visitors to experience the country's stunning scenery while traveling comfortably. The Tren Crucero, a luxurious train journey, takes you on a remarkable adventure from Quito to Guayaquil, passing through the awe-inspiring Andean landscapes, picturesque villages, and lush rainforests. This train ride offers a unique opportunity to witness Ecuador's diverse ecosystems and immerse yourself in its natural wonders.

2. Buses:

Buses are the primary mode of transportation in Ecuador, connecting cities, towns, and rural areas throughout the country. The bus system is well-developed, affordable, and offers a wide range of options to suit different travel preferences. From modern coaches with comfortable seating to smaller local buses, you can choose the level of comfort and convenience that suits your needs. Buses provide an excellent opportunity to interact with locals, experience the authentic culture, and enjoy the breathtaking views along the way.

3. Metros:

Quito, the capital city of Ecuador, is home to an efficient metro system that makes getting around the city a breeze. The Quito Metro, inaugurated in 2020, offers a reliable and eco-friendly mode of transportation, reducing traffic congestion and contributing to a greener environment. With six lines covering various parts of the city, the metro allows you to explore Quito's top attractions, such as the historic center, modern neighborhoods, and vibrant markets, with ease and convenience.

4. Map of Quito's Public Transportation System:

To assist you in navigating Quito's public transportation system, we have included a detailed map in this chapter. This map highlights the metro lines, bus routes, and major train stations, ensuring that you can easily plan your journeys and make the most of your time in the city. Whether you're visiting Quito's iconic landmarks like the Mitad del Mundo or exploring its hidden gems, this map will serve as your reliable companion.

Conclusion:

Ecuador offers a diverse range of public transportation options that cater to the needs of every traveler. Whether you prefer the scenic train journeys, the authentic bus experiences, or the convenience of metros, getting around Ecuador has never been easier. By utilizing the map provided in this chapter, you can confidently explore the stunning landscapes, vibrant cities, and charming towns that make Ecuador a truly remarkable destination. Embark on your journey and immerse yourself in the wonders of this beautiful country, all while minimizing your carbon footprint.

Chapter 15: Types of Accommodation in Ecuador

Introduction:

When planning a trip to Ecuador, one of the most important aspects to consider is the type of accommodation that suits your needs and preferences. Ecuador offers a wide range of options, from luxurious hotels to budget-friendly hostels, charming guesthouses, and unique Airbnbs. In this chapter, we will explore the different types of accommodation available in Ecuador, providing you with insights to make an informed decision for a comfortable and enjoyable stay.

1. Hotels:

Ecuador boasts a diverse selection of hotels, catering to various budgets and preferences. From lavish five-star resorts in the bustling cities of Quito and Guayaquil to cozy boutique hotels nestled in the picturesque towns of Cuenca and Otavalo, there is something for everyone. These accommodations often provide top-notch amenities, including swimming pools, spa facilities, and fine dining options, ensuring a luxurious and relaxing experience.

2. Hostels:

For budget-conscious travelers or those seeking a more social atmosphere, hostels are an excellent choice. Ecuador's hostels are renowned for their affordability, vibrant ambiance, and opportunities to meet fellow travelers from around the world. Many hostels offer shared dormitory-style rooms or private rooms at affordable rates, making them ideal for backpackers and solo adventurers. These accommodations often provide communal spaces, such as lounges, kitchens, and outdoor areas, fostering a sense of community among guests.

3. Guesthouses:

If you are looking for a more intimate and personalized experience, staying in a guesthouse is highly recommended. Ecuadorian guesthouses, often family-run, offer warm hospitality and a glimpse into the local culture. These accommodations are typically smaller in size, providing a cozy and homely atmosphere. Guests can enjoy personalized services, home-cooked meals, and valuable insights from their hosts, creating a more authentic and immersive experience.

4. Airbnbs:

In recent years, Airbnb has gained popularity worldwide, and Ecuador is no exception. Renting an Airbnb allows travelers to experience Ecuador like a local, offering unique and often off-the-beaten-path accommodations. From charming colonial houses in the historic center of Quito to cozy cabins in the lush Amazon rainforest, Airbnb options are diverse and cater to various tastes. Staying in an Airbnb provides the freedom to cook your own meals, enjoy local neighborhoods, and connect with hosts who can offer insider tips and recommendations.

Conclusion:

Choosing the right accommodation is crucial to a memorable and comfortable stay in Ecuador. Whether you prefer the luxury of hotels, the affordability and social atmosphere of hostels, the personalized touch of guesthouses, or the unique experiences offered by Airbnbs, Ecuador has it all. Consider your budget, desired level of comfort, and the type of experience you seek when selecting your accommodation. With the diverse options available, you are sure to find the perfect place to rest and recharge during your Ecuadorian adventure.

Chapter 16: Tips for Staying in Ecuador

Ecuador is a mesmerizing country, known for its diverse landscapes, rich culture, and warm-hearted people. As you embark on your journey to this enchanting destination, it is essential to be well-prepared to make the most out of your stay. In this chapter, we will provide you with valuable tips on booking accommodation, getting around, and staying safe in Ecuador, ensuring a memorable and worry-free experience.

1. Booking Accommodation:

When it comes to booking accommodation in Ecuador, consider the following tips:

a. Research and Compare: Take the time to research different accommodation options, such as hotels, hostels, and eco-lodges. Compare prices, amenities, and reviews to find the best fit for your needs and budget.

b. Location Matters: Choose accommodation that is conveniently located, preferably near public transportation, attractions, and amenities. This will save you time and make your exploration easier.

c. Eco-Friendly Options: Ecuador is a country that values sustainability and ecological preservation. Consider staying in eco-friendly accommodations that promote responsible tourism, such as those certified by the Ministry of Tourism's Sustainable Tourism Certification Program.

2. Getting Around:

To navigate Ecuador efficiently and smoothly, keep the following tips in mind:

a. Public Transportation: Utilize Ecuador's reliable public transportation system, which includes buses, taxis, and trolleybuses. Be cautious while taking taxis and ensure they are metered or negotiate the fare in advance.

b. Domestic Flights: If you plan to explore different regions of Ecuador, consider taking domestic flights. They are relatively affordable and offer breathtaking aerial views of the country's diverse landscapes.

c. Car Rentals: If you prefer more independence and flexibility, renting a car is an option. However, be aware that driving in Ecuador can be challenging due to narrow roads, mountainous terrain, and heavy traffic in urban areas.

3. Staying Safe:

While Ecuador is generally a safe country for tourists, it is crucial to take precautions to ensure your safety:

a. Stay Informed: Stay updated on travel advisories and local news. It is advisable to register with your embassy or consulate before your trip, so they can provide assistance if needed.

b. Avoid Isolated Areas at Night: Like in any other country, it is wise to avoid isolated areas, especially after dark. Stick to well-lit, populated areas and travel in groups whenever possible.

c. Protect Your Belongings: Keep your valuables secure and be cautious of pickpockets in crowded areas. Avoid displaying expensive items and use hotel safes to store your passports, cash, and other important documents.

d. Be Mindful of Scams: Be wary of scams, especially in tourist hotspots. Avoid accepting unsolicited help or engaging in transactions that seem suspicious. Use reputable tour operators and official taxis to minimize the risk of scams.

By following these tips, you can enhance your experience while staying in Ecuador. Remember, being respectful of the local culture, customs, and environment is crucial to ensure a positive and sustainable impact on the country. Enjoy your time in Ecuador and create memories that will last a lifetime!

Chapter 17: Must-See Attractions in Ecuador

Ecuador, a small but incredibly diverse country located in South America, offers a plethora of must-see attractions for travelers seeking adventure, natural beauty, and cultural experiences. From the awe-inspiring Galapagos Islands to the majestic peaks of the Andes Mountains, Ecuador has something to offer every type of traveler. In this chapter, we will explore the top 10 must-see attractions in Ecuador, ensuring that your journey through this remarkable country is both unique and truthful.

1. The Galapagos Islands: A UNESCO World Heritage Site, the Galapagos Islands are a haven for wildlife enthusiasts and nature lovers. Explore the unique ecosystems and encounter species found nowhere else on Earth, such as the famous Galapagos tortoises, marine iguanas, and blue-footed boobies.

2. Quito's Historic Center: Step back in time as you wander through the streets of Quito's Historic Center, a UNESCO World Heritage Site. Admire the well-preserved colonial architecture, visit stunning churches like the Basilica del Voto Nacional, and take in panoramic views of the city from the top of El Panecillo.

3. The Avenue of Volcanoes: Embark on a breathtaking journey through the Avenue of Volcanoes, a stretch of the Andes Mountains where towering peaks dominate the landscape. Cotopaxi, Chimborazo, and Cayambe are just a few of the impressive volcanoes you can explore.

4. The Amazon Rainforest: Immerse yourself in the unparalleled biodiversity of the Amazon Rainforest. Join a guided tour and discover the secrets of this lush ecosystem, encounter vibrant wildlife, and learn about the indigenous communities that call this region home.

5. Cuenca: Known as the Athens of Ecuador Cuenca is a charming colonial city with cobblestone streets, impressive churches, and a

vibrant arts scene. Explore the historic district, visit the iconic blue-domed Cathedral of the Immaculate Conception, and indulge in the local cuisine.

6. The Quilotoa Loop: Hike through the stunning landscapes of the Quilotoa Loop, a series of Andean villages and breathtaking viewpoints surrounding the Quilotoa Crater Lake. Experience the beauty of the Andean highlands and interact with local indigenous communities along the way.

7. Baños: Nestled in the foothills of the Tungurahua volcano, Baños is a paradise for adventure seekers. Enjoy activities such as hiking, mountain biking, and canyoning, or relax in the natural hot springs that the town is famous for.

8. Otavalo Market: Dive into the vibrant colors and rich culture of Ecuador at the Otavalo Market. This indigenous market is one of the largest in South America, offering a wide range of traditional crafts, textiles, and fresh produce.

9. Ingapirca: Explore the ancient Inca ruins of Ingapirca, the largest and best-preserved archaeological site in Ecuador. Discover the fascinating history of the Inca civilization and marvel at the impressive stone structures.

10. Mindo Cloud Forest: Delve into the mystical beauty of the Mindo Cloud Forest, a haven for birdwatchers and nature enthusiasts. Embark on guided hikes, visit butterfly farms, and spot rare species such as the Andean cock-of-the-rock.

These top 10 must-see attractions in Ecuador are just a glimpse of the wonders that await you. Whether you're seeking adventure, cultural immersion, or a deep connection with nature, Ecuador has it all. So pack your bags, embrace the spirit of exploration, and embark on a journey through this enchanting country that will leave you with memories to last a lifetime.

Chapter 18: Natural Wonders of Ecuador

Introduction:

Ecuador, a small country located in the heart of South America, is a land blessed with an extraordinary array of natural wonders. From pristine rainforests to towering volcanoes and stunning coastal landscapes, Ecuador offers a diverse range of breathtaking sights for nature enthusiasts. In this chapter, we will explore the top 10 natural wonders that make Ecuador a true paradise for travelers seeking to connect with the raw beauty of the natural world.

1. The Enchanted Galapagos Islands:

No visit to Ecuador would be complete without a trip to the Galapagos Islands. This archipelago, located in the Pacific Ocean, is renowned for its unique and diverse wildlife. From the giant tortoises to the marine iguanas and blue-footed boobies, the Galapagos Islands offer an unparalleled opportunity to witness evolution in action.

2. The Majestic Cotopaxi Volcano:

Standing tall at 5,897 meters, Cotopaxi is one of the highest active volcanoes in the world. Its perfectly symmetrical cone, covered in snow, is a sight to behold. Adventurous souls can embark on a challenging hike to reach the summit, where they will be rewarded with breathtaking panoramic views of the surrounding landscapes.

3. The Mystical Cloud Forests of Mindo:

Nestled in the Andean foothills, the cloud forests of Mindo are a haven for biodiversity. This mystical ecosystem is home to an incredible variety of flora and fauna, including over 500 species of birds. Nature lovers can explore the lush trails, visit hummingbird sanctuaries, and even experience the thrill of zip-lining through the treetops.

4. The Pristine Amazon Rainforest:

Ecuador is fortunate to have a portion of the Amazon rainforest within its borders. This vast expanse of dense jungle is teeming with life, from colorful birds and elusive jaguars to indigenous communities with rich cultural traditions. Embarking on a guided tour deep into the rainforest is an unforgettable experience, allowing visitors to connect with nature on a profound level.

5. The Breathtaking Quilotoa Crater Lake:

Nestled within the Andes, the Quilotoa Crater Lake is a mesmerizing sight. Its turquoise waters, surrounded by steep cliffs, create a postcard-perfect view. Hiking along the rim of the crater offers stunning vistas, and the more adventurous can descend to the lake's shore for a refreshing swim.

6. The Spectacular Avenue of the Volcanoes:

Stretching for over 300 kilometers, the Avenue of the Volcanoes is a captivating sight. This scenic route is flanked by towering peaks, including the iconic Cotopaxi, Chimborazo, and Tungurahua volcanoes. Driving through this volcanic corridor offers a unique opportunity to witness the raw power and beauty of these natural wonders.

7. The Charming Quilotoa Loop:

For those seeking an off-the-beaten-path adventure, the Quilotoa Loop is a must. This remote region, located in the central highlands, offers breathtaking vistas of the Andean countryside. Visitors can hike through traditional indigenous villages, witness local customs, and marvel at the stunning landscapes that unfold at every turn.

8. The Serene Cajas National Park:

Located near the city of Cuenca, Cajas National Park is a haven of tranquility. This high-altitude park is dotted with over 200 glacial lakes, creating a surreal landscape. Hiking through the park's trails allows visitors to immerse themselves in the pristine beauty of the Andean highlands.

9. The Exquisite Yasuni National Park:

Yasuni National Park, located in the Ecuadorian Amazon, is a UNESCO Biosphere Reserve and one of the most biodiverse places on Earth. This untouched wilderness is home to countless species, including the elusive pink river dolphins and the vibrant poison dart frogs. Exploring the park's waterways and lush forests is a true immersion into the wonders of the natural world.

10. The Magnificent El Cajas National Park:

El Cajas National Park, located just outside of Guayaquil, is a paradise for nature lovers. This high-altitude park is characterized by its rugged terrain, crystal-clear lakes, and unique páramo vegetation. Hiking through the park's trails offers a chance to spot Andean condors soaring overhead and to witness the resilience of life in extreme environments.

Conclusion:

Ecuador's natural wonders are as diverse as the country itself. From the enchanting Galapagos Islands to the pristine Amazon rainforest, this small nation offers an extraordinary range of experiences for those seeking to connect with nature. Whether you're an avid hiker, a wildlife enthusiast, or simply someone who appreciates the beauty of the natural world, Ecuador's top 10 natural wonders are sure to leave you in awe.

Chapter 19: Historical and Cultural Sites in Ecuador

Introduction:

Ecuador, a small country located in South America, is bursting with rich history and vibrant culture. From ancient ruins to colonial cities, Ecuador offers a diverse range of historical and cultural sites that will leave any traveler in awe. In this chapter, we will explore the top 10 historical and cultural sites in Ecuador, each offering a unique glimpse into the country's past and present.

1. Quito's Historic Center:

Begin your journey in Ecuador's capital, Quito, and immerse yourself in its charming historic center. Declared a UNESCO World Heritage Site, this well-preserved colonial quarter boasts stunning architecture, narrow cobblestone streets, and beautiful churches such as the iconic Basílica del Voto Nacional and the breathtaking Compañía de Jesús.

2. Ingapirca:

Located in the Cañar Province, Ingapirca is the country's most important Inca archaeological site. Explore the ruins of this ancient complex, including the elliptical Sun Temple and the Temple of the Moon. Admire the intricate stonework and learn about the Inca civilization's influence in Ecuador.

3. Cuenca's Historic Center:

Cuenca, another UNESCO World Heritage Site, is a city renowned for its well-preserved colonial architecture. Stroll along its cobblestone streets, visit the impressive Catedral de la Inmaculada Concepción, and explore the many museums showcasing Ecuadorian art and history.

4. Galapagos Islands:

While primarily known for their unique wildlife, the Galapagos Islands also hold historical significance. Discover the Charles Darwin Research Station on Santa Cruz Island, where you can learn about the naturalist's studies and conservation efforts. Explore the Galapagos National Park, a living testament to Ecuador's commitment to preserving its natural and cultural heritage.

5. Otavalo Market:

Venture to the town of Otavalo and experience one of the largest indigenous markets in South America. This vibrant market showcases traditional crafts, textiles, and local produce. Engage with the locals, learn about their customs, and perhaps take home a beautiful handmade souvenir.

6. Cajas National Park:

Escape into the stunning landscapes of Cajas National Park, located near Cuenca. This protected area is not only a paradise for nature enthusiasts but also holds archaeological sites that reveal the ancient cultures that once inhabited the region. Explore the pristine lakes, hike through the high-altitude páramo, and uncover the remnants of Ecuador's past.

7. San Francisco Church, Quito:

Visit the San Francisco Church, a true gem in Quito's historic center. This 16th-century church showcases an exquisite blend of Spanish, Moorish, and indigenous architectural styles. Marvel at the intricate gold leaf decorations inside the church and explore the adjacent museum, which houses an impressive collection of religious art.

8. Mindo Cloud Forest:

Embark on a journey to the enchanting Mindo Cloud Forest, a haven for birdwatchers and nature lovers. While exploring the lush greenery, visit the Butterfly Garden and the Hummingbird Sanctuary, where you can witness Ecuador's incredible biodiversity up close.

9. Museo del Banco Central, Quito:

Delve into Ecuador's pre-Columbian history at the Museo del Banco Central in Quito. This museum houses an extensive collection of artifacts, including pottery, jewelry, and tools from various indigenous cultures. Gain a deeper understanding of Ecuador's diverse heritage and the importance of preserving its cultural legacy.

10. Puerta de la Ciudad, Cuenca:

End your journey in Cuenca by visiting the iconic Puerta de la Ciudad, a grand entrance gate to the city. This symbolic structure represents the city's historical significance and is a testament to Ecuador's rich cultural heritage.

Conclusion:

Ecuador's historical and cultural sites offer a fascinating glimpse into the country's past and present. From ancient ruins to colonial cities, each destination showcases unique facets of Ecuadorian history and culture. Immerse yourself in the vibrant atmosphere, explore the architectural wonders, and engage with the locals to truly appreciate the beauty and significance of these top 10 historical and cultural sites in Ecuador.

Chapter 20: Museums and Art Galleries in Ecuador

Introduction:

Ecuador, a country known for its rich cultural heritage and diverse history, is home to numerous museums and art galleries that offer a glimpse into its past and present. From ancient artifacts to contemporary art, these institutions provide visitors with a unique opportunity to explore Ecuador's artistic and cultural expressions. In this chapter, we will take you on a journey through the top 10 museums and art galleries in Ecuador, each offering a distinct experience that showcases the country's artistic and historical treasures.

1. Museo del Banco Central del Ecuador, Quito:

Located in the heart of Quito, the Museo del Banco Central del Ecuador houses an extensive collection of pre-Columbian, colonial, and contemporary art. With over 5,000 artifacts, including ceramics, textiles, and gold objects, this museum offers a comprehensive overview of Ecuador's rich cultural heritage.

2. Museo Antropológico y de Arte Contemporáneo, Guayaquil:

Situated in Guayaquil, the Museo Antropológico y de Arte Contemporáneo is a must-visit for art enthusiasts. Its collection includes both national and international contemporary artworks, showcasing the diversity and creativity of Ecuadorian artists.

3. Museo de Arte Moderno, Cuenca:

Nestled in the charming city of Cuenca, the Museo de Arte Moderno is dedicated to promoting modern and contemporary art in Ecuador. With a focus on local artists, this museum offers a unique perspective on the country's artistic evolution.

4. Museo de la Ciudad, Quito:

The Museo de la Ciudad, located in Quito's historic center, provides visitors with a fascinating journey through the city's history.

Through interactive exhibits and multimedia displays, this museum brings to life the stories of Quito's past, making it a must-visit for history enthusiasts.

5. Museo Nacional del Ecuador, Quito:

As the largest museum in Ecuador, the Museo Nacional del Ecuador offers a comprehensive overview of the country's history and culture. From archaeological artifacts to colonial art, this museum provides visitors with a deep understanding of Ecuador's past.

6. Centro Cultural Metropolitano, Quito:

Housed in a beautifully restored colonial building, the Centro Cultural Metropolitano is a vibrant cultural hub in Quito. With rotating exhibitions featuring both local and international artists, this art gallery offers a dynamic and ever-changing experience for visitors.

7. Museo de la Ciudad, Guayaquil:

Situated in a former hospital building, the Museo de la Ciudad in Guayaquil showcases the city's history through a diverse range of exhibits. From archaeological finds to historical documents, this museum provides a comprehensive understanding of Guayaquil's past.

8. Casa de la Cultura Ecuatoriana, Quito:

The Casa de la Cultura Ecuatoriana is a cultural institution that promotes and preserves Ecuador's artistic heritage. With multiple art galleries showcasing various art forms, including painting, sculpture, and photography, this cultural center is a haven for art lovers.

9. Museo de las Conceptas, Cuenca:

Located within a former convent, the Museo de las Conceptas in Cuenca offers a unique glimpse into the lives of the nuns who once resided there. With its well-preserved colonial architecture and religious artifacts, this museum provides a fascinating insight into Ecuador's colonial past.

10. Museo de Arte Precolombino Casa del Alabado, Quito:

Dedicated to the pre-Columbian art of Ecuador, the Museo de Arte Precolombino Casa del Alabado houses a remarkable collection of ancient artifacts. From intricate ceramics to precious gold pieces, this museum offers a captivating exploration of Ecuador's indigenous cultures.

Conclusion:

Ecuador's museums and art galleries are a testament to the country's rich cultural heritage and artistic expressions. From ancient artifacts to contemporary masterpieces, these institutions provide visitors with a unique opportunity to delve into Ecuador's history and immerse themselves in its vibrant art scene. Whether you are a history buff or an art enthusiast, a visit to these top 10 museums and art galleries in Ecuador is sure to leave you with a deeper appreciation for the country's cultural tapestry.

Chapter 21: Religious Sites in Ecuador

Introduction:

Ecuador, a country nestled in the heart of South America, is not only known for its breathtaking landscapes and rich biodiversity but also for its deep-rooted religious traditions. With a diverse population, Ecuador is home to numerous religious sites that hold great significance for both locals and visitors alike. In this chapter, we will explore the top 10 religious sites in Ecuador, each offering a unique insight into the country's spiritual heritage.

1. Basilica del Voto Nacional, Quito:

Located in the heart of Quito, the Basilica del Voto Nacional stands tall as a testament to Ecuador's Catholic faith. This neo-Gothic masterpiece not only showcases stunning architecture but also offers visitors an opportunity to climb to the top of its towers for panoramic views of the city.

2. La Compania de Jesus, Quito:

Considered one of the most beautiful churches in South America, La Compania de Jesus is a Baroque masterpiece that mesmerizes visitors with its intricate gold leaf decorations. Its awe-inspiring interior is a true testament to the craftsmanship of Ecuadorian artisans.

3. El Cajas National Park, Cuenca:

While not a traditional religious site, El Cajas National Park offers a unique spiritual experience for nature lovers. Its serene landscapes, crystal-clear lakes, and mystical cloud forests provide a tranquil environment for meditation and self-reflection.

4. Ingapirca, Cañar Province:

As Ecuador's most important Inca ruins, Ingapirca holds great historical and religious significance. Visitors can explore the Temple of the Sun, a sacred site where ancient rituals were performed, and learn about the fusion of Inca and Spanish cultures.

5. Basílica de Nuestra Señora de Las Lajas, Ipiales:

Located just across the border from Ecuador in Colombia, the Basílica de Nuestra Señora de Las Lajas is a stunning Gothic-style church built on a bridge over a gorge. It is believed to be a place of miraculous healings and attracts pilgrims from all over the world.

6. Santuario de la Virgen del Rocio, Guayaquil:

Nestled in the vibrant city of Guayaquil, the Santuario de la Virgen del Rocio is a popular pilgrimage site for Catholics. The sanctuary houses a statue of the Virgin Mary, which is believed to have performed miracles, and offers a serene atmosphere for prayer and reflection.

7. San Francisco Church, Quito:

Dating back to the 16th century, the San Francisco Church is one of Quito's oldest and most significant religious sites. Its stunning architecture, including its iconic yellow facade, and rich history make it a must-visit for those interested in Ecuador's colonial past.

8. Capilla del Hombre, Quito:

The Capilla del Hombre, or Chapel of Man, is a unique museum and art space dedicated to the works of renowned Ecuadorian artist Oswaldo Guayasamín. This spiritual sanctuary showcases Guayasamín's powerful paintings, which depict the struggles and resilience of the human spirit.

9. El Quinche, Pichincha Province:

El Quinche is a small town known for its religious celebrations and the Basilica of the National Shrine of Our Lady of El Quinche. Every year, thousands of pilgrims flock to this site to pay homage to the patron saint of Ecuador, Our Lady of El Quinche.

10. La Catedral de la Inmaculada Concepcion, Cuenca:

Cuenca's grand cathedral, also known as the New Cathedral, is a magnificent example of Ecuadorian Gothic architecture. Its towering blue domes and intricate stained glass windows create a captivating atmosphere for worship and reflection.

Conclusion:

Ecuador's religious sites offer a captivating blend of history, spirituality, and cultural heritage. Whether you seek architectural marvels, natural sanctuaries, or places of pilgrimage, these top 10 religious sites in Ecuador are sure to leave a lasting impression on your journey through this diverse and enchanting country.

Chapter 22: Outdoor Activities in Ecuador

Introduction:

Ecuador, a small yet diverse country located in South America, is a haven for adventure enthusiasts and nature lovers. With its breathtaking landscapes, including the Andean mountains, the Amazon rainforest, and the Galapagos Islands, Ecuador offers a plethora of outdoor activities for visitors to enjoy. In this chapter, we will explore the top 10 outdoor activities in Ecuador, providing you with unique and truthful insights to make the most of your adventure-filled journey.

1. Hiking the Quilotoa Loop:

Embark on a multi-day hiking adventure through the Quilotoa Loop, a trail that takes you through remote Andean villages, lush valleys, and stunning volcanic landscapes. Witness the beauty of the Quilotoa crater lake and immerse yourself in the local culture and traditions along the way.

2. Whitewater Rafting in the Amazon:

Experience the thrill of navigating the rapids of the Amazon River, surrounded by the pristine beauty of the rainforest. Whitewater rafting in the Amazon allows you to witness Ecuador's incredible biodiversity while enjoying an adrenaline-pumping adventure.

3. Mountain Biking in Baños:

Explore the charming town of Baños on two wheels, as you navigate through its scenic landscapes and waterfalls. Mountain biking in Baños offers an exhilarating way to discover hidden gems, such as the Pailon del Diablo waterfall, while enjoying breathtaking views of the Tungurahua volcano.

4. Surfing in Montañita:

Head to the vibrant coastal town of Montañita, known as the surfing capital of Ecuador. Whether you are a beginner or an experienced surfer, Montañita's consistent waves and lively atmosphere make it the perfect destination for riding the waves and soaking up the sun.

5. Trekking the Avenue of the Volcanoes:

Embark on a trek along the Avenue of the Volcanoes, a stretch of the Andean highlands dotted with majestic volcanoes. This trek offers stunning views of snow-capped peaks, picturesque valleys, and the opportunity to summit some of Ecuador's highest mountains, such as Cotopaxi and Chimborazo.

6. Paragliding in Quito:

Soar above the cityscape of Quito, the capital of Ecuador, as you engage in the thrilling activity of paragliding. Enjoy panoramic views of the Andean mountains and the city's historic center, a UNESCO World Heritage site, while experiencing the ultimate rush of adrenaline.

7. Wildlife Watching in the Galapagos Islands:

Embark on a once-in-a-lifetime adventure to the Galapagos Islands, a UNESCO World Heritage site and a haven for unique wildlife species. Observe Galapagos giant tortoises, marine iguanas, blue-footed boobies, and other endemic species while snorkeling, hiking, and cruising around the archipelago.

8. Canyoning in Mindo:

Discover the hidden treasures of Mindo's cloud forest through canyoning, an exciting activity that involves rappelling down waterfalls and exploring the lush canyons. Immerse yourself in the natural beauty of this biodiverse region as you navigate through its cascading waterfalls and crystal-clear pools.

9. Horseback Riding in the Andes:

Saddle up and explore the Andean highlands on horseback, following ancient trails that lead to remote indigenous communities and breathtaking landscapes. Horseback riding in the Andes allows you to connect with Ecuador's rich cultural heritage while enjoying the tranquility of its scenic countryside.

10. Zip-lining in Mindo Cloud Forest:

Experience an adrenaline rush as you zip-line through the misty cloud forest of Mindo, soaring above the treetops and marveling at the lush greenery. This thrilling activity provides a unique perspective of the forest's diverse flora and fauna while offering an unforgettable adventure.

Conclusion:

Ecuador's natural wonders and diverse landscapes provide endless opportunities for outdoor activities. From hiking and biking to surfing and wildlife watching, this chapter has highlighted the top 10 outdoor activities in Ecuador, ensuring that you can explore the country's beauty while indulging in thrilling adventures. Remember to respect and preserve Ecuador's natural environment as you embark on these activities, leaving only footprints and taking away memories that will last a lifetime.

Chapter 23: Shopping in Ecuador

Introduction:

Ecuador, a country known for its rich cultural heritage and stunning landscapes, also offers a vibrant shopping scene. From bustling markets to upscale boutiques, Ecuador has something for every type of shopper. In this chapter, we will explore the best places to shop in Ecuador and highlight some of the unique products you can find.

1. Otavalo Market:

Located in the highlands of Ecuador, the Otavalo Market is a must-visit for any shopaholic. This world-renowned market is famous for its vibrant textiles, hand-woven rugs, and intricately crafted jewelry. As you stroll through the market, you will be captivated by the vibrant colors and exquisite craftsmanship of the products. Don't forget to haggle for the best prices!

2. Quito's Old Town:

Quito, the capital city of Ecuador, is a UNESCO World Heritage site and home to a plethora of shopping opportunities. The Old Town, in particular, is a treasure trove for shoppers. Here, you will find quaint boutiques selling traditional Ecuadorian clothing, leather goods, and unique handicrafts. Take your time to explore the narrow cobblestone streets and discover hidden gems.

3. La Ronda Street:

Situated in the heart of Quito's historic district, La Ronda Street is a charming pedestrian-only street lined with shops and cafes. This picturesque street is known for its artisanal products, such as handmade ceramics, wooden crafts, and traditional musical instruments. As you wander through the shops, you can witness local artisans at work, creating beautiful pieces right before your eyes.

4. Cuenca's Artisan Market:

Cuenca, a city in southern Ecuador, is famous for its thriving artisan community. The Artisan Market in Cuenca is a haven for those seeking authentic Ecuadorian crafts. From alpaca wool sweaters and Panama hats to intricate pottery and silver jewelry, you will find it all here. The market is also a great place to interact with local artisans and learn about their craft.

5. Galapagos Islands Souvenirs:

If you're visiting the Galapagos Islands, don't miss the opportunity to bring back unique souvenirs. The islands offer a range of locally made products, including hand-painted t-shirts, eco-friendly jewelry made from sustainable materials, and intricate seashell crafts. These souvenirs not only serve as mementos but also contribute to supporting the local economy and conservation efforts.

Conclusion:

Shopping in Ecuador is a delightful experience that allows you to immerse yourself in the country's vibrant culture and support local artisans. Whether you're exploring the bustling markets of Otavalo, wandering through the historic streets of Quito, or seeking authentic crafts in Cuenca, you'll find an array of unique products to take home. Remember to haggle for the best prices and enjoy the thrill of discovering hidden treasures. Happy shopping!

Chapter 24: Nightlife in Ecuador

Ecuador is not only known for its stunning natural landscapes and cultural heritage but also for its vibrant and diverse nightlife. Whether you are a party animal or seeking a tranquil evening, Ecuador has something to offer for everyone. From lively clubs to cozy bars and traditional dance halls, this chapter will guide you through the best places to go out at night in Ecuador. Get ready to immerse yourself in the country's rich nightlife scene and discover the tips for enjoying an unforgettable evening.

1. Quito's Historic Center: A Night of Culture and Fun

The capital city, Quito, boasts a remarkable historic center that comes alive at night. Begin your evening with a visit to La Ronda, a charming street filled with traditional taverns, live music, and local artisans. Savor delicious Ecuadorian cuisine and try chicha, a traditional corn-based drink. As the night progresses, head to Plaza Foch, known for its lively clubs and bars, where you can dance the night away to Latin rhythms or enjoy live performances by local bands.

2. Guayaquil's Malecon 2000: A Modern Waterfront Experience

Guayaquil, Ecuador's largest city, offers a modern and cosmopolitan nightlife experience. Start your evening at Malecon 2000, a scenic waterfront promenade lined with trendy bars and restaurants. Enjoy a cocktail while taking in the breathtaking views of the Guayas River. For a unique experience, visit the Las Peñas neighborhood, known for its bohemian atmosphere and vibrant nightlife. Explore its narrow streets filled with art galleries, cafes, and live music venues.

3. Montañita: A Beach Town Party Paradise

For those seeking a lively beach town atmosphere, Montañita is the place to be. Located on the Pacific coast, this small town is famous for its surfing waves during the day and its vibrant nightlife after sundown. Stroll along the main street, Calle de los Cocteles, where you will find an array of bars and clubs offering tropical cocktails and pulsating beats. Dance until dawn with locals and fellow travelers, creating memories that will last a lifetime.

4. Cuenca's Traditional Dance Halls: A Cultural Night Out

Cuenca, a UNESCO World Heritage Site, invites you to experience its traditional dance halls known as peñas. These venues offer a unique opportunity to immerse yourself in Ecuadorian folklore and traditional music. Enjoy live performances of Andean music and witness traditional dances such as the Sanjuanito and the Pasillo. Indulge in local delicacies while sipping on canelazo, a warm spiced drink. The peñas of Cuenca provide an authentic and memorable night out for those seeking a cultural experience.

Tips for Enjoying the Nightlife in Ecuador:

1. Safety First: Like in any other country, it is essential to prioritize your safety. Always be aware of your surroundings, avoid walking alone at night, and take registered taxis when needed.

2. Dress Code: While Ecuador is generally casual, some clubs and upscale establishments may enforce a dress code. It's best to dress smart-casual to ensure entry into any venue.

3. Local Recommendations: Don't hesitate to ask locals or fellow travelers for recommendations. They can provide valuable insights into hidden gems and the latest hotspots in town.

4. Pace Yourself: Ecuadorians love to party, but it's important to pace yourself and drink responsibly. Stay hydrated and know your limits to fully enjoy the night without any regrets.

5. Embrace the Culture: Ecuador's nightlife is a perfect opportunity to embrace the local culture. Try traditional drinks, dance to local rhythms, and engage with the friendly locals. It will enhance your overall experience and create lasting memories.

As you explore the nightlife in Ecuador, remember to respect the local customs and enjoy the unique experiences each destination offers. From lively cities to tranquil beach towns, Ecuador's nightlife scene has something for everyone. So, get ready to dance, mingle, and create unforgettable memories in this vibrant country.

Chapter 25: Festivals and Events in Ecuador

Introduction:

Ecuador, a country nestled in the heart of South America, is known for its rich cultural heritage and vibrant traditions. Throughout the year, Ecuadorians celebrate various festivals and events that showcase their deep-rooted customs, colorful costumes, and lively music. This chapter will guide you through the calendar of major festivals and events in Ecuador, offering a unique opportunity to immerse yourself in the country's vibrant culture.

1. Inti Raymi - The Festival of the Sun (June 24th):

One of the most significant festivals in Ecuador, Inti Raymi, pays homage to the sun god, Inti. Celebrated on June 24th, this ancient Incan festival takes place in the highlands of Ecuador, particularly in the city of Otavalo. Locals dress in traditional attire and gather to honor Inti through music, dance, and offerings. Witnessing the vibrant procession and the ceremonial rituals is a truly unforgettable experience.

2. Fiesta de la Mama Negra - The Festival of the Black Madonna (September 23rd):

Originating from the city of Latacunga, this unique festival combines indigenous, African, and Spanish traditions. The Fiesta de la Mama Negra celebrates the Black Madonna, a revered figure in Ecuadorian folklore. The festival features colorful parades, traditional dances, and street performances. Locals dress up as Mama Negra, donning extravagant costumes and masks, while the streets come alive with music and fireworks.

3. Carnival - The Festival of Water and Flour (February/March):

Ecuadorians eagerly await the arrival of Carnival, a joyous celebration that takes place in various cities and towns across the country. This festival signals the beginning of Lent and is characterized by water fights, flour battles, and vibrant parades. Expect to be drenched in water and covered in flour as locals and tourists alike join in the spirited revelry. Carnival is a time of laughter, music, and uninhibited fun.

4. La Diablada de Píllaro - The Devil's Dance (January 1st):

In the small town of Píllaro, located in the central highlands of Ecuador, the streets come alive with the mesmerizing La Diablada. This festival blends indigenous and Spanish traditions, featuring dancers dressed as devils, angels, and other mythical creatures. The vibrant masks and costumes, accompanied by traditional music and dance, create an enchanting spectacle that symbolizes the eternal battle between good and evil.

5. Corpus Christi - The Festival of Corpus Christi (May/June):

Quito, the capital city of Ecuador, hosts one of the most important religious festivals in the country, Corpus Christi. This festival celebrates the Catholic belief in the body and blood of Christ. Elaborate processions fill the streets, with participants carrying religious statues adorned with flowers and accompanied by traditional music. The festival provides a fascinating insight into Ecuador's religious devotion and cultural heritage.

Conclusion:

Ecuador's calendar is brimming with festivals and events that offer a glimpse into the country's rich cultural tapestry. From ancient Incan rituals to vibrant street celebrations, each festival provides a unique and truthful experience. Immerse yourself in the lively music, colorful costumes, and warm hospitality of the Ecuadorian people as you partake in these unforgettable cultural celebrations.

Chapter 26: Activities for Couples in Ecuador

Ecuador, a country known for its stunning landscapes, rich culture, and diverse wildlife, offers an array of romantic activities for couples to enjoy. Whether you are seeking adventure, relaxation, or cultural experiences, Ecuador has it all. Here are the top 10 most romantic activities for couples in Ecuador:

1. Explore the Enchanted Galapagos Islands: Embark on a once-in-a-lifetime adventure to the Galapagos Islands, where you and your partner can witness unique wildlife, snorkel with sea turtles, and walk hand in hand on pristine beaches.

2. Wander through Quito's Old Town: Take a stroll through Quito's historic center, a UNESCO World Heritage site, and get lost in its charming cobblestone streets, colonial architecture, and vibrant plazas. Enjoy a romantic dinner at one of the many cozy restaurants offering traditional Ecuadorian cuisine.

3. Relax in the Hot Springs of Baños: Located in the heart of the Andes Mountains, Baños is famous for its rejuvenating hot springs. Indulge in a relaxing soak with your loved one while surrounded by breathtaking natural scenery.

4. Horseback Riding in the Andes: Explore the picturesque landscapes of the Andes Mountains on horseback. Enjoy the breathtaking views, lush valleys, and snow-capped peaks as you ride alongside your partner, creating memories that will last a lifetime.

5. Sunset Cruise in the Galapagos: Set sail on a romantic sunset cruise around the Galapagos Islands. Witness the vibrant colors of the sky as the sun sets over the Pacific Ocean, while enjoying a glass of champagne and a delicious dinner.

6. Chocolate Tasting in Mindo: Discover the magic of Ecuadorian chocolate in the cloud forest town of Mindo. Take a tour of a chocolate

factory, learn about the production process, and savor the flavors of high-quality Ecuadorian chocolate together.

7. Hiking in Cotopaxi National Park: Lace up your hiking boots and embark on a romantic adventure in Cotopaxi National Park. Explore the stunning landscapes, hike to the base of the Cotopaxi volcano, and enjoy a picnic surrounded by nature.

8. Birdwatching in the Cloud Forest: Immerse yourselves in the enchanting cloud forest of Mindo, a paradise for birdwatchers. Wake up early to catch a glimpse of colorful hummingbirds, toucans, and other exotic bird species in their natural habitat.

9. Take a Romantic Train Ride: Hop aboard the Tren Crucero, a luxury train that traverses the Andes, offering breathtaking views of Ecuador's diverse landscapes. Enjoy a romantic journey together, savoring delicious meals and immersing yourselves in the country's rich history.

10. Visit the Quilotoa Crater Lake: Take a day trip to the Quilotoa Crater Lake, known for its mesmerizing turquoise waters. Hike down to the lake's shore with your partner, or simply admire the view from the rim while enjoying a romantic picnic.

Remember, Ecuador offers countless romantic activities for couples to enjoy. Whether you prefer adventure, relaxation, or cultural experiences, this diverse country has something to offer every couple seeking a memorable and romantic getaway.

Chapter 27: Activities for Solo Travelers in Ecuador

Introduction:

Ecuador, a diverse and vibrant country in South America, offers a plethora of activities for solo travelers seeking adventure, cultural immersion, and natural wonders. This chapter will guide you through the top ten activities that are perfect for solo travelers in Ecuador. From exploring the Amazon rainforest to wandering through colonial cities, Ecuador has something for everyone.

1. Galapagos Islands Exploration:

Embark on a unique solo adventure by visiting the Galapagos Islands, a UNESCO World Heritage site. Discover the enchanting wildlife, including giant tortoises, marine iguanas, and blue-footed boobies, while snorkeling, hiking, or cruising around the archipelago. Dive into the crystal-clear waters and witness the incredible underwater world, making this an unforgettable experience for any solo traveler.

2. Quito City Tour:

Explore the historic center of Quito, the capital city of Ecuador, which is a UNESCO World Heritage site. Wander through its charming streets, visit impressive churches, and marvel at the colonial architecture. Take a cable car ride to the top of the Pichincha Volcano for breathtaking panoramic views of the city and its surrounding mountains.

3. Mindo Cloud Forest Adventure:

Escape to the lush Mindo Cloud Forest, located just a few hours from Quito. As a solo traveler, you can immerse yourself in nature by hiking through the cloud forest, observing exotic bird species, and experiencing thrilling activities such as canopy zip-lining and tubing down the rivers. Don't miss the chance to visit a local chocolate factory and indulge in delicious organic chocolate.

4. Cotopaxi National Park Trek:

Challenge yourself with a solo trek in Cotopaxi National Park, home to the magnificent Cotopaxi Volcano. Hike through the beautiful Andean landscapes, spot wildlife like wild horses and llamas, and reach the base camp of the volcano. If you're an experienced climber, you can even attempt to summit this active volcano, making it an unforgettable adventure for solo travelers seeking a physical and mental challenge.

5. Baños de Agua Santa:

Visit the adventure capital of Ecuador, Baños de Agua Santa, nestled in the Andean mountains. As a solo traveler, you can enjoy adrenaline-pumping activities such as canyoning, white-water rafting, and bungee jumping. Don't forget to relax in the natural hot springs and admire the breathtaking views of the Tungurahua Volcano.

6. Amazon Rainforest Expedition:

Embark on a solo journey into the heart of the Amazon rainforest, one of the most biodiverse places on Earth. Stay at an eco-lodge and immerse yourself in the jungle, guided by experienced local naturalists. Explore the lush vegetation, spot wildlife like monkeys and colorful birds, and learn about the indigenous communities that call the rainforest their home.

7. Otavalo Indigenous Market:

Experience the vibrant culture of Ecuador by visiting the famous Otavalo Indigenous Market, the largest indigenous market in South America. As a solo traveler, you can wander through the bustling stalls, admire the traditional handicrafts, and interact with the friendly locals. Don't miss the opportunity to purchase unique souvenirs, such as handmade textiles and jewelry.

8. Cuenca City Exploration:

Discover the colonial charm of Cuenca, a UNESCO World Heritage city renowned for its well-preserved architecture and rich cultural heritage. As a solo traveler, you can explore the cobblestone streets, visit impressive museums, and indulge in the local gastronomy. Don't forget to climb to the top of Turi Hill for a panoramic view of the city.

9. Quilotoa Loop Trek:

Embark on a solo trek along the Quilotoa Loop, a scenic route that takes you through indigenous communities and stunning landscapes. Hike around the mesmerizing Quilotoa Crater Lake, known for its turquoise waters, and spend the night in charming guesthouses along the way. This off-the-beaten-path adventure offers a unique opportunity to connect with nature and local culture.

10. Montañita Beach Experience:

End your solo adventure in Ecuador by relaxing on the beautiful beaches of Montañita. Known for its vibrant surf culture, this coastal town offers a laid-back atmosphere, perfect for unwinding and meeting fellow travelers. Enjoy the world-class waves, indulge in fresh seafood, and dance the night away at beachside parties.

Conclusion:

Ecuador is a dream destination for solo travelers, offering a diverse range of activities that cater to every interest. From exploring the unique wildlife of the Galapagos Islands to embarking on thrilling adventures in the Andean mountains, Ecuador has it all. Embrace the freedom of solo travel and immerse yourself in the natural wonders, rich culture, and warm hospitality that this incredible country has to offer.

Chapter 28: Budget-friendly activities in Ecuador

Introduction:

Ecuador, a vibrant South American country, offers a plethora of budget-friendly activities for travelers seeking to explore its natural wonders, cultural heritage, and diverse landscapes. In this chapter, we will delve into the top 10 budget-friendly activities that will allow you to make the most of your time in Ecuador without breaking the bank.

1. Hiking in the Andes:

Embark on an unforgettable adventure by exploring the Andes Mountains. With numerous hiking trails, such as the Quilotoa Loop and Cotopaxi National Park, you can witness breathtaking landscapes, encounter indigenous communities, and marvel at majestic volcanoes, all without spending a fortune.

2. Exploring Quito's Historic Center:

Discover the rich history and architectural wonders of Quito's Historic Center, a UNESCO World Heritage Site. Stroll through its cobblestone streets, visit iconic landmarks like the Plaza de la Independencia and the Basilica del Voto Nacional, and immerse yourself in the vibrant local culture, all at no cost.

3. Wildlife Spotting in the Galapagos Islands:

While visiting the Galapagos Islands may seem expensive, there are budget-friendly ways to experience its unique wildlife. Join day tours from Santa Cruz Island to explore the pristine beaches, swim with sea lions, and observe marine iguanas and giant tortoises in their natural habitats.

4. Relaxing in Baños de Agua Santa:

Unwind in the charming town of Baños de Agua Santa, known for its hot springs and picturesque landscapes. Take a dip in the thermal baths, hike to the stunning Pailon del Diablo waterfall, or rent a bike to explore the surrounding countryside, all at affordable prices.

5. Visiting Otavalo Market:

Immerse yourself in Ecuador's indigenous culture by visiting the famous Otavalo Market. Located just a few hours from Quito, this vibrant market offers a wide array of traditional crafts, textiles, and handmade souvenirs at reasonable prices. Don't forget to haggle for the best deals!

6. Trekking in the Amazon Rainforest:

Embark on an unforgettable adventure into the heart of the Amazon Rainforest. Join budget-friendly jungle tours from towns like Tena or Puyo, where you can explore the lush jungle, spot exotic wildlife, and learn about indigenous communities and their sustainable way of life.

7. Surfing in Montañita:

Head to the coastal town of Montañita, known as Ecuador's surf capital, for an affordable beach getaway. Whether you're a seasoned surfer or a beginner, you can rent a board, take lessons, and catch some waves in this laid-back and budget-friendly destination.

8. Discovering Cuenca's Colonial Charm:

Explore the colonial city of Cuenca, renowned for its well-preserved historic center and impressive architecture. Wander through its narrow streets, visit the Cathedral of the Immaculate Conception, and admire the iconic blue-domed churches, all while enjoying the city's affordable food and accommodation options.

9. Biking the Avenue of the Volcanoes:

Embark on a budget-friendly biking adventure along the Avenue of the Volcanoes, a scenic route flanked by towering volcanoes. Rent a bike in Riobamba or Latacunga and pedal through picturesque landscapes, passing by stunning peaks like Cotopaxi and Chimborazo.

10. Relaxing on the Pacific Coast:

Unwind on Ecuador's Pacific Coast, where you'll find budget-friendly beach towns like Canoa and Puerto Lopez. Enjoy long stretches of sandy beaches, indulge in fresh seafood, and even partake in whale watching during certain seasons, all while keeping your travel expenses in check.

Conclusion:

Ecuador offers an abundance of budget-friendly activities for travelers with a sense of adventure and a desire to explore its natural wonders and cultural heritage. From hiking in the Andes to discovering the Galapagos Islands on a budget, this chapter has provided you with an array of truthful and unique experiences that will make your trip to Ecuador unforgettable without straining your wallet.

Chapter 29: Off-the-Beaten-Path Activities in Ecuador

Introduction:

Ecuador, a small yet diverse country located in South America, offers a plethora of off-the-beaten-path activities for adventurous travelers seeking unique experiences. From exploring hidden natural wonders to immersing in local culture, this chapter will uncover the top 10 off-the-beaten-path activities in Ecuador. Get ready to embark on an extraordinary journey through Ecuador's lesser-known gems.

1. Trekking in the Cloud Forests of Mindo:

Escape the crowds and venture into the mystical cloud forests of Mindo. This off-the-beaten-path destination offers an array of hiking trails, leading you to mesmerizing waterfalls, vibrant bird species, and lush vegetation. Immerse yourself in the tranquility of nature as you explore this hidden gem.

2. Discovering the Lost City of Ingapirca:

Unearth the secrets of Ingapirca, Ecuador's most significant Inca archaeological site. Located in the Andean highlands, this off-the-beaten-path destination allows you to explore ancient ruins, including the Temple of the Sun and the elliptical-shaped Castle. Immerse yourself in history as you unravel the mysteries of this captivating site.

3. Snorkeling with Marine Life in Machalilla National Park:

Escape the touristy spots and head to Machalilla National Park for an unforgettable snorkeling experience. Dive into the crystal-clear waters, where you'll encounter a diverse range of marine life, including sea turtles, colorful fish, and even manta rays. This off-the-beaten-path activity promises an up-close encounter with Ecuador's underwater wonders.

4. Exploring the Cajas National Park:

For nature enthusiasts seeking solitude, Cajas National Park is a must-visit off-the-beaten-path destination. Located near Cuenca, this unique ecosystem offers breathtaking landscapes, dotted with over 200 glacial lakes and rolling hills. Hike through the park's trails, spot unique bird species, and immerse yourself in the serenity of this hidden gem.

5. Experiencing Indigenous Culture in Otavalo:

Escape the tourist crowds and delve into the rich indigenous culture of Otavalo. This off-the-beaten-path destination is renowned for its vibrant markets, where you can purchase traditional handicrafts directly from local artisans. Immerse yourself in the colorful textiles, intricate jewelry, and delicious traditional cuisine, all while supporting the local community.

6. Horseback Riding in the Andean Highlands:

Embark on a unique horseback riding adventure through the picturesque landscapes of the Andean Highlands. This off-the-beaten-path activity allows you to connect with nature while riding through lush valleys, crossing rivers, and encountering indigenous communities along the way. Experience Ecuador's natural beauty from a different perspective.

7. Exploring the Underground Caves of Jumandy:

Unleash your inner explorer and venture into the underground caves of Jumandy. Located in the Amazon Rainforest, this off-the-beaten-path activity takes you on a thrilling journey through dark tunnels, underground rivers, and fascinating rock formations. Discover the hidden wonders that lie beneath the surface of Ecuador's diverse ecosystem.

8. Birdwatching in the Yasuni National Park:

Escape the tourist trails and immerse yourself in the biodiversity of Yasuni National Park. This off-the-beaten-path destination is a paradise for birdwatchers, boasting over 600 bird species, including the iconic Amazonian parrot. Join a guided tour and spot colorful feathered creatures in their natural habitat, surrounded by the sounds of the rainforest.

9. Surfing in Canoa:

For those seeking an off-the-beaten-path beach experience, Canoa is the perfect destination. This laid-back coastal town offers uncrowded waves, making it an ideal spot for surfers of all levels. Enjoy the tranquility of the beach, catch some waves, and soak up the sun in this hidden gem on Ecuador's Pacific coast.

10. Exploring the El Angel Ecological Reserve:

Uncover the enchanting beauty of the El Angel Ecological Reserve, a hidden gem located in the northern highlands of Ecuador. This off-the-beaten-path destination is known for its unique páramo ecosystem, featuring unique vegetation and stunning landscapes. Hike through the reserve's trails, encounter unique plant species, and marvel at the mystical beauty of this untouched wilderness.

Conclusion:

Ecuador's off-the-beaten-path activities offer a glimpse into the country's hidden treasures. From exploring cloud forests and ancient ruins to snorkeling with marine life and immersing in indigenous culture, this chapter has revealed the top 10 unique and truthful off-the-beaten-path activities in Ecuador. Embark on these extraordinary adventures and create memories that will last a lifetime.

Chapter 30: Sustainable Tourism Experiences in Ecuador

Introduction:

Ecuador, a country known for its incredible biodiversity and stunning landscapes, has emerged as a pioneer in sustainable tourism. This chapter will highlight the top 10 sustainable tourism experiences in Ecuador, where travelers can immerse themselves in the country's natural wonders while contributing to its conservation efforts. From the enchanting Galapagos Islands to the lush Amazon rainforest, Ecuador offers a range of eco-friendly experiences that showcase the country's commitment to preserving its unique ecosystems.

1. Exploring the Galapagos Islands:

The Galapagos Islands, a UNESCO World Heritage Site, are a haven for wildlife enthusiasts. Travelers can embark on eco-friendly cruises and guided tours that adhere to strict environmental regulations. These experiences offer an up-close encounter with iconic species like the Galapagos giant tortoise, marine iguanas, and blue-footed boobies, while simultaneously educating visitors about the importance of conservation.

2. Trekking in the Andes:

Ecuador's Andean region is home to breathtaking landscapes and vibrant indigenous cultures. Travelers can embark on sustainable trekking adventures, such as the famous Quilotoa Loop or the Cotopaxi National Park. These experiences not only provide an opportunity to hike amidst stunning scenery but also support local communities by staying in eco-lodges and purchasing handmade crafts directly from artisans.

3. Volunteering in the Amazon Rainforest:

For those seeking a more immersive experience, volunteering in the Amazon rainforest is an excellent way to contribute to its conservation.

Various organizations offer volunteer programs focused on reforestation, wildlife monitoring, and sustainable community development. Participants can engage in hands-on activities while learning about the region's delicate ecosystem and the challenges it faces.

4. Community-based Tourism in the Cloud Forest:

Ecuador's cloud forest is a unique ecosystem teeming with endemic species and lush vegetation. Travelers can opt for community-based tourism experiences, staying in eco-lodges owned and operated by local communities. These experiences provide an intimate insight into the region's biodiversity, as well as opportunities to learn traditional practices, such as coffee production or medicinal plant usage, directly from the locals.

5. Responsible Whale Watching in Puerto Lopez:

The coastal town of Puerto Lopez offers a sustainable whale-watching experience that supports the conservation of humpback whales. Visitors can join responsible tour operators who adhere to strict guidelines to minimize disturbance to these majestic creatures. Through educational programs and scientific research, travelers can actively contribute to the protection of these endangered marine mammals.

6. Sustainable Farm Stays in the Andean Highlands:

Ecuador's Andean highlands are dotted with picturesque farms where travelers can experience sustainable agriculture firsthand. By staying at eco-friendly farm stays, visitors can participate in organic farming practices, learn about traditional agricultural techniques, and savor farm-to-table meals prepared with locally sourced ingredients. These experiences promote sustainable livelihoods for local farmers and encourage the preservation of traditional farming methods.

7. Conservation Projects in the Galapagos Marine Reserve:

For passionate marine conservationists, participating in conservation projects within the Galapagos Marine Reserve is a unique opportunity. Travelers can join research teams to monitor marine species, assist in coral reef restoration efforts, and contribute to the ongoing protection of this fragile ecosystem. These hands-on experiences allow visitors to actively contribute to the preservation of the Galapagos Islands' marine biodiversity.

8. Sustainable City Tours in Quito:

Ecuador's capital city, Quito, offers sustainable city tours that showcase its rich history and cultural heritage. Travelers can explore the city's colonial center, a UNESCO World Heritage Site, while learning about sustainable urban development initiatives. These tours often include visits to community projects, such as urban gardens and recycling centers, highlighting Quito's commitment to becoming a sustainable city.

9. Birdwatching in Mindo:

Mindo, a small town nestled in the cloud forest, is a paradise for birdwatchers. Travelers can engage in sustainable birdwatching tours led by knowledgeable local guides who emphasize the importance of conservation. These experiences offer a chance to spot rare and colorful bird species while supporting local efforts to protect their habitats.

10. Responsible Wildlife Photography in the Yasuni National Park:

Yasuni National Park, located in the Ecuadorian Amazon, is a biodiverse hotspot renowned for its wildlife. Travelers can participate in responsible wildlife photography workshops led by professional photographers who prioritize animal welfare and environmental ethics. By capturing the beauty of the park's flora and fauna, visitors can raise awareness about the importance of preserving this unique ecosystem.

Conclusion:

Ecuador's commitment to sustainable tourism is evident in its diverse range of eco-friendly experiences. Whether exploring the Galapagos Islands, trekking in the Andes, or volunteering in the Amazon rainforest, travelers can actively contribute to the conservation of Ecuador's natural wonders. By choosing sustainable tourism experiences, visitors can enjoy the country's breathtaking landscapes while leaving a positive impact on its environment and communities.

Chapter 31: Responsible Tourism Experiences in Ecuador

Introduction:

Ecuador, known for its breathtaking landscapes, diverse wildlife, and rich cultural heritage, offers travelers a unique opportunity to engage in responsible tourism experiences. By choosing responsible tourism, visitors can contribute to the preservation of Ecuador's natural and cultural treasures while positively impacting local communities. In this chapter, we will explore the top 10 responsible tourism experiences in Ecuador, ensuring an unforgettable and sustainable journey.

1. Exploring the Galápagos Islands:

Embark on a responsible adventure to the Galápagos Islands, where you can witness the incredible biodiversity that inspired Charles Darwin's theory of evolution. Choose eco-friendly tour operators that prioritize conservation efforts and adhere to strict guidelines to protect the fragile ecosystem of this UNESCO World Heritage Site.

2. Community-Based Tourism in the Amazon Rainforest:

Immerse yourself in the enchanting Amazon Rainforest by participating in community-based tourism initiatives. Stay with local indigenous communities, learn about their traditions, and engage in sustainable activities such as wildlife spotting, medicinal plant workshops, and responsible fishing practices. Your visit will directly support these communities' efforts to preserve their ancestral lands.

3. Sustainable Farm Stays in the Andean Highlands:

Experience the traditional way of life in the Andean Highlands by staying at sustainable farms. Learn about organic farming practices, participate in traditional cooking classes, and engage in cultural exchanges with local communities. These farm stays provide economic opportunities for rural populations while preserving the region's unique cultural heritage.

4. Wildlife Conservation in the Cloud Forest:

Visit the captivating cloud forests of Ecuador and contribute to wildlife conservation efforts. Join responsible eco-lodges and organizations that work towards protecting endangered species such as the elusive Andean spectacled bear and the vibrant bird populations. Participate in research projects, guided hikes, and reforestation activities, leaving a positive impact on these fragile ecosystems.

5. Responsible Volunteering in the Galápagos National Park:

For those seeking a more immersive experience, consider volunteering in the Galápagos National Park. Assist park rangers in conservation projects, such as eradicating invasive species, monitoring wildlife populations, and educating visitors about sustainable practices. Your contribution will directly support the preservation of this unique archipelago.

6. Cultural Exchanges with Indigenous Communities:

Engage in cultural exchanges with Ecuador's indigenous communities, such as the Kichwa, Shuar, and Huaorani. Stay in community-run accommodations, learn traditional crafts, participate in rituals, and listen to ancestral stories. These interactions provide economic empowerment for indigenous groups while fostering cultural understanding and appreciation.

7. Responsible Diving in the Pacific Coast:

Discover the wonders of Ecuador's Pacific Coast through responsible diving practices. Choose dive centers that prioritize marine conservation and adhere to strict guidelines to protect fragile coral reefs and marine life. Dive alongside giant manta rays, sea turtles, and colorful fish, while supporting ongoing research and conservation efforts.

8. Sustainable City Tours in Quito and Cuenca:

Explore the historic cities of Quito and Cuenca through sustainable city tours. Choose local tour operators that focus on responsible tourism practices, emphasizing the preservation of architectural heritage and supporting local artisans. Discover hidden gems, taste traditional cuisine, and learn about the cities' cultural significance while contributing to their sustainable development.

9. Responsible Adventure Tourism in Baños:

Experience the adrenaline rush of adventure tourism in Baños, while choosing responsible operators that prioritize safety and environmental conservation. Engage in activities such as canyoning, zip-lining, and biking, all while supporting local communities and contributing to the protection of natural resources.

10. Sustainable Wildlife Rehabilitation Centers:

Visit wildlife rehabilitation centers in Ecuador, dedicated to rescuing and rehabilitating animals affected by illegal wildlife trade or habitat destruction. Learn about the challenges faced by these species and the conservation efforts being made to protect them. Your visit and support will directly contribute to the rehabilitation and release of these animals back into the wild.

Conclusion:

By engaging in responsible tourism experiences in Ecuador, you have the power to make a positive impact on the country's natural and cultural heritage. Choose tour operators and accommodations that prioritize sustainability, support local communities, and contribute to conservation efforts. By doing so, you can ensure a truly unique, truthful, and responsible journey through Ecuador.

Chapter 32: Volunteer Opportunities in Ecuador

Introduction:

Ecuador, a country known for its incredible biodiversity and stunning landscapes, offers a plethora of volunteer opportunities for those seeking to make a positive impact while exploring this enchanting destination. Whether you have a passion for wildlife conservation, community development, or environmental sustainability, Ecuador has something to offer everyone. In this chapter, we will delve into the top ten volunteer opportunities in Ecuador, providing you with unique and truthful insights to help you make an informed decision.

1. Galapagos Islands Conservation:

Embark on a once-in-a-lifetime journey to the Galapagos Islands and contribute to the preservation of this UNESCO World Heritage Site. Volunteer programs focus on protecting the unique flora and fauna, conducting research, and educating visitors about sustainable practices.

2. Amazon Rainforest Conservation:

Immerse yourself in the heart of the Amazon rainforest and join efforts to protect this vital ecosystem. Volunteers can participate in reforestation projects, wildlife research, and community-based initiatives aimed at promoting sustainable livelihoods.

3. Andean Community Development:

Experience the rich culture and traditions of indigenous communities in the Andes while supporting their development. Volunteer programs focus on education, healthcare, infrastructure, and empowering local artisans to preserve their traditional crafts.

4. Coastal Marine Conservation:

If you have a passion for marine life, consider volunteering along Ecuador's stunning coastline. Help protect endangered species, such as sea turtles, by monitoring nesting sites, raising awareness about conservation, and participating in beach clean-ups.

5. Sustainable Agriculture:

Ecuador's fertile lands provide an excellent opportunity to engage in sustainable agriculture practices. Volunteers can work alongside local farmers, learning about organic farming techniques, promoting food security, and supporting fair trade initiatives.

6. Environmental Education:

Make a difference in the lives of Ecuadorian children by volunteering in environmental education programs. Teach them about the importance of conservation, sustainable practices, and inspire the next generation of environmental stewards.

7. Wildlife Rehabilitation:

If you have a passion for animal welfare, consider volunteering at wildlife rehabilitation centers. Assist in the rescue, rehabilitation, and release of injured or confiscated animals, such as monkeys, birds, and reptiles, while promoting their conservation.

8. Sustainable Tourism:

Contribute to the growth of responsible tourism in Ecuador by volunteering with organizations focused on sustainable tourism practices. Help develop community-based tourism initiatives, promote cultural exchange, and minimize the environmental impact of tourism activities.

9. English Language Teaching:

Volunteer your time and skills to teach English in local schools and community centers. By improving English proficiency, you can empower Ecuadorian individuals to access better employment opportunities and broaden their horizons.

10. Climate Change Research:

Join scientific research projects focused on understanding and mitigating the impacts of climate change in Ecuador. Assist in data collection, analysis, and the development of strategies to promote resilience and adaptation.

Conclusion:

Ecuador provides a myriad of volunteer opportunities that allow you to contribute meaningfully to the country's environmental and social well-being. From the enchanting Galapagos Islands to the lush Amazon rainforest and vibrant Andean communities, each experience offers a unique chance to make a positive impact while immersing yourself in Ecuador's rich culture and natural wonders. Choose the opportunity that resonates with your interests and values, and embark on a transformative journey of volunteering in Ecuador.

Chapter 33: Visas and Immigration Requirements for Ecuador

Introduction:

Welcome to Chapter 33 of our tourist guide, where we will provide you with a comprehensive summary of the visa and immigration requirements for visiting Ecuador. It is essential to familiarize yourself with these regulations to ensure a smooth and hassle-free entry into this beautiful country. Please note that the information provided here is accurate at the time of writing, but it is always advisable to check with the relevant authorities or consult your embassy for the most up-to-date information.

1. Tourist Visa:

Ecuador offers a generous tourist visa policy, allowing citizens of many countries to enter without a visa for varying periods. Citizens from countries such as the United States, Canada, the United Kingdom, Australia, and most European nations can enter Ecuador as tourists for up to 90 days within a one-year period. This visa is typically granted upon arrival at the airport or any official border crossing point. However, it is important to check if your nationality requires a visa in advance or if any specific conditions apply.

2. Passport Requirements:

To enter Ecuador, your passport must be valid for at least six months beyond your intended stay. Ensure that your passport has enough blank pages for entry and exit stamps. It is always wise to carry a photocopy of your passport's main page and keep it separate from the original document for security purposes.

3. Visa Extensions:

If you wish to extend your stay beyond the initial 90 days, you can apply for an extension at the Ministry of Foreign Affairs in Ecuador. The extension can be granted for an additional 90 days, but it is subject to approval and may require presenting a valid reason for the extension.

4. Business Visa:

If you are planning to conduct business activities in Ecuador, such as attending conferences, meetings, or exploring potential investment opportunities, you may need to apply for a business visa. This type of visa requires additional documentation, including an invitation letter from a local company or organization, proof of financial means, and a detailed itinerary of your business activities. It is advisable to consult with the Ecuadorian embassy or consulate in your home country to determine the specific requirements for obtaining a business visa.

5. Work Visa:

If you intend to work in Ecuador, you must obtain a work visa before entering the country. The process for obtaining a work visa can be complex and requires sponsorship from an Ecuadorian employer. The employer will need to submit various documents, including a formal job offer, proof of their company's registration, and evidence that no local candidates are available for the position. It is highly recommended to consult with a local immigration attorney or the Ecuadorian embassy in your home country to navigate this process effectively.

Conclusion:

Understanding the visa and immigration requirements for Ecuador is crucial to ensure a smooth entry and stay in the country. This chapter has provided you with an overview of the tourist visa policy, passport requirements, visa extensions, as well as information on business and work visas. Remember to always check for updates and consult the relevant authorities or your embassy for the most accurate and up-to-date information. Enjoy your time exploring the wonders of Ecuador!

Chapter 34: Money and Banking in Ecuador

Introduction:

Welcome to the vibrant and diverse country of Ecuador! In this chapter, we will explore the intricacies of money and banking in Ecuador, providing you with essential information on the local currency, exchange rates, ATMs, and credit cards. Understanding these aspects will ensure a smooth financial experience during your travels. So, let's dive into the fascinating world of Ecuadorian currency!

1. The Ecuadorian Currency:

The official currency of Ecuador is the United States dollar (USD). Since 2000, Ecuador has adopted the US dollar as its legal tender, making it convenient for travelers from the United States and other countries using the dollar. You can rest assured that your dollar bills will be widely accepted throughout the country.

2. Exchange Rates:

As the US dollar is the official currency, there are no exchange rates to consider within Ecuador. However, it is advisable to check the current exchange rates in your home country before arriving in Ecuador to have a better understanding of the value of your money.

3. ATMs in Ecuador:

ATMs are readily available in major cities and tourist destinations in Ecuador. They accept international debit and credit cards, allowing you to withdraw US dollars or the local currency, known as the sucre. It is important to note that some ATMs may charge a small fee for each transaction, so be sure to check with your bank regarding any potential fees before traveling.

4. Credit Cards:

Credit cards, especially Visa and Mastercard, are widely accepted in hotels, restaurants, and larger establishments throughout Ecuador.

However, it is always wise to carry some cash for smaller vendors and local markets, as they might not have card payment facilities.

5. Safety and Precautions:

While Ecuador is generally safe for tourists, it is essential to take precautions to protect your money and personal information. Avoid displaying large sums of cash in public, be cautious when using ATMs in secluded areas, and keep an eye on your surroundings to prevent any potential theft or scams. Additionally, inform your bank about your travel plans to avoid any unexpected card issues.

6. Currency Exchange:

If you prefer to exchange your money in person, there are currency exchange offices available in major cities and airports. It is advisable to compare exchange rates and fees before making any transactions to ensure you receive the best value for your money.

7. Traveler's Checks:

While traveler's checks were once a popular option for tourists, their usage has significantly declined in recent years. It may be challenging to find establishments that accept traveler's checks in Ecuador. Therefore, it is recommended to rely on a combination of cash and cards for your financial needs.

Conclusion:

Having a good understanding of money and banking in Ecuador will undoubtedly enhance your travel experience. With the US dollar as the official currency, ATMs readily available, and credit cards widely accepted, managing your finances will be a breeze. Remember to prioritize safety and take necessary precautions to safeguard your money while exploring the enchanting wonders of Ecuador.

Chapter 35: Communication in Ecuador

Introduction:

Ecuador, a mesmerizing country known for its diverse landscapes and rich cultural heritage, offers a range of communication facilities to keep both locals and tourists connected. In this chapter, we will explore the phone system, internet access, and postal service in Ecuador, providing you with essential information to stay connected during your visit.

1. The Phone System:

Ecuador boasts a well-developed phone system that ensures reliable communication across the country. The main service providers are CNT, Movistar, and Claro, offering both mobile and landline services. To make local calls within Ecuador, simply dial the seven-digit phone number. For international calls, dial the country code followed by the area code and the desired number. It is advisable to purchase a local SIM card for your mobile phone to enjoy affordable rates and seamless connectivity during your stay.

2. Internet Access:

Staying connected online is crucial for travelers, and Ecuador offers various options for internet access. Most hotels, hostels, and cafes provide free Wi-Fi services, allowing you to connect your devices easily. Additionally, you can find internet cafes in major cities and tourist destinations where you can access the internet for a small fee. If you require constant internet access, portable Wi-Fi devices are available for rent, ensuring uninterrupted connectivity as you explore the country.

3. Postal Service:

Sending postcards or packages to your loved ones from Ecuador is a delightful way to share your travel experiences. The Ecuadorian postal service, Correos del Ecuador, efficiently handles domestic and international mail. Post offices can be found in major cities, and postage stamps can be purchased at these locations. It is advisable to check the weight and size restrictions for international packages to ensure hassle-free delivery. Alternatively, courier services such as DHL and FedEx are also available for faster and more secure shipping options.

4. Internet Cafes and Communication Centers:

In addition to Wi-Fi services, internet cafes and communication centers are prevalent throughout Ecuador. These establishments offer computer rentals, printing, scanning, and fax services, ensuring you have access to various communication tools. Additionally, some centers provide international calling booths, allowing you to make affordable international calls to stay connected with loved ones back home.

5. Language Barrier:

While communication facilities are readily available in Ecuador, it is important to note that Spanish is the official language. English proficiency among locals may vary, particularly in remote areas. However, in popular tourist destinations and major cities, you can find individuals who speak English, making it easier to communicate. Learning a few basic Spanish phrases can greatly enhance your ability to interact with locals and navigate through the country.

Conclusion:

Communication in Ecuador is reliable and accessible, ensuring that you can stay connected during your visit. With a well-developed phone system, widespread internet access, and efficient postal services, you can easily share your experiences and keep in touch with loved ones. Embrace the opportunity to learn some basic Spanish phrases, as it will undoubtedly enhance your overall experience and interactions with the warm and welcoming people of Ecuador.

Chapter 36: Health and Safety in Ecuador

Introduction:

As you embark on your journey through the beautiful landscapes and vibrant culture of Ecuador, it is essential to prioritize your health and safety. This chapter aims to provide you with an overview of common health risks in Ecuador and offer practical safety tips to ensure a memorable and worry-free experience.

Common Health Risks:

1. Altitude Sickness:

Ecuador's diverse geography includes high-altitude regions such as Quito and the Andean mountains. Altitude sickness, also known as soroche, can affect individuals who are not acclimatized to higher elevations. Symptoms may include headaches, dizziness, nausea, and shortness of breath. To prevent altitude sickness, it is recommended to gradually ascend to higher altitudes, stay well-hydrated, and avoid excessive physical exertion during the first few days.

2. Food and Water Safety:

While Ecuador offers a delightful culinary experience, it is crucial to be cautious about food and water hygiene. To avoid stomach ailments, it is advisable to consume bottled or purified water, thoroughly wash fruits and vegetables, and opt for well-cooked meals. Street food can be tempting, but it is wise to choose vendors with high customer turnover and observe their food handling practices.

3. Mosquito-Borne Diseases:

Ecuador is home to various mosquito-borne diseases, including dengue fever, Zika virus, and malaria. To minimize the risk of mosquito bites, use insect repellents containing DEET, wear long-sleeved clothing, and sleep under mosquito nets, especially in areas with higher mosquito activity. Consult with a healthcare professional before your trip to discuss any necessary vaccinations or preventive medications.

4. Sun Exposure:

Ecuador's proximity to the equator means that the sun's intensity is stronger, increasing the risk of sunburn and heatstroke. Protect yourself by wearing sunscreen with a high SPF, a wide-brimmed hat, sunglasses, and lightweight, breathable clothing. Seek shade during the peak hours of sunlight and stay hydrated to prevent dehydration.

Safety Tips:

1. Personal Safety:

Ecuador, like any other destination, has its share of petty theft and scams. It is advisable to remain vigilant in crowded areas, keep your belongings secure, and avoid displaying valuable items. Use reputable transportation services and be cautious when using ATMs. Consider purchasing travel insurance to cover any unforeseen circumstances.

2. Natural Hazards:

Ecuador is prone to natural disasters such as earthquakes and volcanic eruptions. Stay informed about potential risks by monitoring local news and adhering to any evacuation procedures if necessary. Familiarize yourself with emergency contact numbers and have a plan in place in case of an emergency.

3. Transportation Safety:

When traveling within Ecuador, prioritize your safety by using licensed and reputable transportation services. Be cautious on public buses, especially at night, and consider using registered taxis or ride-sharing apps. If renting a vehicle, ensure you have the necessary permits and insurance coverage.

Conclusion:

By being aware of the common health risks and following the safety tips provided in this chapter, you can enjoy your time in Ecuador with peace of mind. Remember to consult with healthcare professionals, research your destination, and exercise caution to ensure a safe and healthy adventure in this captivating country.

Chapter 37: Travel Insurance for Ecuador

Introduction:

Traveling to Ecuador is an exciting adventure filled with vibrant culture, breathtaking landscapes, and unique experiences. However, it is important to be prepared for any unforeseen circumstances that may arise during your trip. This is where travel insurance comes into play. In this chapter, we will explore the benefits of travel insurance for Ecuador and guide you on how to purchase the right coverage for your needs.

Understanding the Benefits of Travel Insurance:

1. Medical Coverage:

One of the primary benefits of travel insurance is medical coverage. In Ecuador, while healthcare facilities are available, they may not meet the same standards as in your home country. Travel insurance ensures that you have access to quality medical care in case of illness or injury during your trip.

2. Trip Cancellation or Interruption:

Life is unpredictable, and sometimes unforeseen circumstances can force you to cancel or cut short your trip to Ecuador. Travel insurance provides coverage for trip cancellation or interruption due to reasons such as illness, injury, or even natural disasters, ensuring you don't suffer financial losses.

3. Emergency Evacuation:

Ecuador is known for its diverse landscapes, including the Galapagos Islands and the Amazon rainforest. However, these remote areas may pose challenges in case of emergencies. Travel insurance offers emergency evacuation coverage, ensuring that you can be transported to the nearest suitable medical facility if needed.

4. Lost or Delayed Luggage:

Traveling to Ecuador often involves multiple flights or transfers. Unfortunately, lost or delayed luggage can disrupt your travel plans. Travel insurance provides coverage for lost or delayed luggage, allowing you to replace essential items and continue your journey without unnecessary stress.

5. Personal Liability:

Accidents can happen, even while traveling. Travel insurance offers personal liability coverage, protecting you from potential legal expenses if you accidentally cause damage to property or harm someone else during your trip.

How to Purchase Travel Insurance for Ecuador:

1. Research:

Start by researching different travel insurance providers to find the one that offers comprehensive coverage specifically tailored for travel to Ecuador. Look for companies that have a good reputation and positive customer reviews.

2. Evaluate Coverage:

Carefully evaluate the coverage options offered by different insurance providers. Ensure that the policy covers medical expenses, trip cancellation, emergency evacuation, lost luggage, and personal liability. Additionally, check for any exclusions or limitations that may affect your specific travel plans.

3. Compare Quotes:

Obtain quotes from multiple insurance providers and compare the cost of coverage. While price is important, ensure that you are not compromising on coverage and benefits for the sake of a cheaper policy.

4. Read the Fine Print:

Before purchasing travel insurance, read the policy documents thoroughly. Understand the terms and conditions, including any deductibles, claim processes, and emergency contact information. If you have any questions, reach out to the insurance provider for clarification.

5. Purchase Early:

It is advisable to purchase travel insurance as soon as you book your trip to Ecuador. This ensures that you are covered for any unexpected events that may occur before your departure.

Conclusion:

Travel insurance is an essential component of any trip to Ecuador. It provides peace of mind and financial protection against unforeseen circumstances. By understanding the benefits of travel insurance and following the steps outlined in this chapter, you can purchase the right coverage for your Ecuadorian adventure. Remember, being prepared allows you to fully immerse yourself in the beauty and wonders of this captivating country.

Chapter 38: Learning the Language of Ecuador

Introduction:

Learning the language of a foreign country enhances your travel experience by allowing you to communicate effectively with locals and immerse yourself in the local culture. In Ecuador, the official language is Spanish, and gaining a basic understanding of it will open doors to meaningful interactions and enrich your journey. This chapter will provide you with a summary of the resources available for learning the language of Ecuador, ensuring an authentic and unique experience during your visit.

1. Language Schools:

Ecuador boasts numerous language schools that cater to travelers seeking to learn Spanish. These schools offer a variety of courses, ranging from intensive programs to flexible schedules, accommodating learners of all levels. Some renowned language schools include the Simon Bolivar Spanish School in Quito and the Montañita Spanish School in Montañita. These institutions provide qualified teachers, cultural activities, and a friendly environment conducive to language acquisition.

2. Online Language Learning Platforms:

For those who prefer a more flexible approach to learning, online language learning platforms can be an excellent resource. Websites like Duolingo, Babbel, and Rosetta Stone offer comprehensive Spanish courses that can be accessed from anywhere, at any time. These platforms utilize interactive exercises, quizzes, and audiovisual materials to facilitate language learning, making it an accessible and convenient option for travelers exploring Ecuador.

3. Language Exchange Programs:

Immersing yourself in the local culture is an effective way to learn a language, and language exchange programs provide a unique opportunity for just that. In Ecuador, you can find language exchange programs where locals interested in learning English or other languages are eager to exchange conversations with travelers looking to practice Spanish. Websites like ConversationExchange.com and Tandem facilitate language exchanges and help connect language learners in Ecuador.

4. Language Learning Apps:

In the digital era, language learning apps have gained popularity due to their convenience and -friendly interfaces. Apps like Memrise, HelloTalk, and FluentU offer a wide range of Spanish lessons, vocabulary building exercises, and real-life conversations to enhance your language skills. These apps often provide offline accessibility, making them ideal companions for travelers exploring different regions of Ecuador.

5. Cultural Immersion:

One of the most effective ways to learn a language is through cultural immersion. While traveling in Ecuador, take advantage of every opportunity to engage with locals, whether it be in markets, restaurants, or local events. By actively participating in the daily life of Ecuadorians, you will gain exposure to the language, develop your conversational skills, and acquire a deeper understanding of the local culture.

Conclusion:

Learning the language of Ecuador is a valuable investment that will greatly enhance your travel experience. Whether you choose to enroll in a language school, utilize online platforms, engage in language exchange programs, or immerse yourself in the local culture, the resources available ensure a unique and authentic journey. Embrace the opportunity to communicate with Ecuadorians in their native language, and you will forge meaningful connections, gain insights, and create memories that will last a lifetime.

Chapter 39: Tips for Traveling with Children in Ecuador

Introduction:

Traveling with children can be an exciting and rewarding experience, especially when exploring a country as diverse and breathtaking as Ecuador. This chapter aims to provide parents and guardians with valuable tips on how to make their trip to Ecuador with children a memorable and enjoyable adventure. From packing essentials to family-friendly accommodations and engaging activities, this guide will ensure a hassle-free and fun-filled vacation for the whole family.

What to Pack:

1. Comfortable Clothing: Ecuador's climate varies greatly, so pack a mix of lightweight clothing for warmer regions and warmer layers for cooler areas like the Andes. Don't forget raincoats and waterproof shoes for unexpected showers.

2. Sun Protection: Ecuador's proximity to the equator means stronger sun rays. Pack sunscreen, hats, and sunglasses to protect your little ones from harmful UV rays.

3. Medications and First Aid Kit: Include any necessary medications, such as motion sickness or allergies, and a basic first aid kit for minor injuries.

4. Snacks and Water: Keep your children energized and hydrated during outings by packing their favorite snacks and a refillable water bottle.

Where to Stay:

1. Family-Friendly Hotels: Look for accommodations that cater to families, offering amenities like spacious rooms, cribs, high chairs, and play areas. Many hotels in Ecuador, especially in popular tourist destinations, have dedicated family-friendly facilities.

2. Vacation Rentals: Consider renting a family-friendly apartment or house, which often provides more space and a kitchenette for preparing meals. This option allows you to maintain a routine and cater to specific dietary needs.

3. Eco-Lodges: Ecuador is known for its eco-friendly initiatives. Choose to stay in an eco-lodge that offers educational programs and activities for children, promoting environmental awareness and appreciation.

Things to Do:

1. Explore Quito's Historic Center: Take a stroll through Quito's UNESCO World Heritage-listed historic center, where your children can marvel at the stunning colonial architecture, visit museums, and interact with street performers.

2. Discover the Galapagos Islands: Embark on a family-friendly cruise or opt for day tours to explore the unique wildlife and landscapes of the Galapagos Islands. Snorkeling with sea lions and observing giant tortoises are experiences your children will never forget.

3. Visit Otavalo Market: Take a trip to the famous Otavalo Market, known for its vibrant colors and traditional crafts. Let your children explore the market, interact with local artisans, and even learn to haggle for souvenirs.

4. Experience the Amazon Rainforest: Immerse your family in the wonders of the Amazon Rainforest. Choose a lodge that offers guided nature walks, canoe trips, and opportunities to spot exotic wildlife like monkeys, birds, and butterflies.

Conclusion:

Traveling with children in Ecuador can be an enriching experience for the whole family. By following these tips, you can ensure a smooth and enjoyable trip, packed with unforgettable adventures and opportunities for cultural exchange. Remember to prioritize your children's needs, engage them in the planning process, and embrace the wonders of Ecuador together.

Chapter 40: Tips for Traveling with Seniors in Ecuador

Introduction:

Traveling with seniors can be a rewarding and memorable experience, especially in a country as diverse and breathtaking as Ecuador. This chapter aims to provide you with valuable tips and insights to ensure a smooth and enjoyable trip for both you and your elderly loved ones. From packing essentials to suitable accommodations and exciting activities, let us guide you on how to make the most of your journey through Ecuador.

1. Planning and Preparation:

a) Consult with a healthcare professional: Before embarking on your trip, it is essential to seek advice from your loved one's healthcare provider. They can offer valuable insights into any necessary vaccinations, medication adjustments, or precautions to consider.

b) Research and choose suitable destinations: Ecuador offers a wide range of attractions, but it is crucial to select destinations that cater to the needs and abilities of your senior companion. Opt for places with accessible infrastructure, moderate climates, and a slower pace of life.

2. Packing Essentials:

a) Medications and medical documents: Ensure an ample supply of any prescribed medications, along with copies of medical records, insurance information, and emergency contact numbers.

b) Comfortable clothing and footwear: Pack loose-fitting, breathable clothing suitable for the varying climates in Ecuador. Sturdy, comfortable shoes with good traction are essential for exploring different terrains.

c) Sun protection: Ecuador's proximity to the equator means intense sunlight. Pack wide-brimmed hats, sunglasses, and high SPF sunscreen to protect against harmful UV rays.

d) Snacks and water: Keep a stock of healthy snacks and bottled water to keep your loved one hydrated and energized during your explorations.

3. Accommodations:

a) Accessible accommodations: When booking accommodations, prioritize places that offer accessible rooms, elevators, and handrails for added safety and convenience.

b) Proximity to amenities: Choose accommodations within close proximity to medical facilities, restaurants, and attractions to minimize travel time and ensure easy access to necessary services.

4. Transportation:

a) Choose comfortable modes of transportation: Opt for comfortable vehicles or public transportation options that offer ample legroom, seat belts, and air conditioning.

b) Plan for breaks: Frequent breaks during long journeys can help alleviate any discomfort or fatigue experienced by seniors. Plan for rest stops and opportunities to stretch their legs.

5. Sightseeing and Activities:

a) Pace yourselves: It is essential to plan your itinerary with a slower pace in mind. Allow for plenty of breaks and relaxation time to ensure your senior companion can fully enjoy each experience.

b) Choose accessible attractions: Ecuador offers a variety of attractions suitable for seniors, such as botanical gardens, museums, and scenic drives. Ensure these destinations are accessible and have facilities for resting and refreshments.

c) Guided tours: Consider booking guided tours that cater specifically to seniors, as they often provide knowledgeable guides, accessible routes, and transportation options tailored to their needs.

Conclusion:

Traveling with seniors in Ecuador can be an enriching and fulfilling experience for both you and your loved ones. By following these tips, you can ensure a safe, comfortable, and unforgettable journey.

Remember to plan meticulously, choose suitable accommodations, pack wisely, and tailor your activities to suit the abilities and preferences of your senior companion. Embrace the beauty of Ecuador together and create cherished memories that will last a lifetime.

Chapter 41: Tips for Traveling Solo in Ecuador

Introduction:

Traveling solo can be an incredibly rewarding experience, allowing you to immerse yourself in new cultures, meet interesting people, and create lifelong memories. Ecuador, with its stunning landscapes, rich history, and vibrant culture, is an ideal destination for solo travelers. This chapter will provide you with valuable tips on where to stay, things to do, and how to stay safe while exploring this diverse South American country.

Where to Stay:

1. Hostels: Ecuador offers a wide range of hostels that cater to solo travelers. These budget-friendly accommodations not only provide a comfortable stay but also offer opportunities to meet fellow adventurers. Some popular hostels in Quito, the capital city, include Community Hostel, Secret Garden Quito, and The Blue Door Housing.

2. Homestays: For a more immersive experience, consider staying with a local family through a homestay program. This allows you to learn about Ecuadorian traditions, practice your Spanish, and gain a deeper understanding of the country's culture. Websites like Airbnb and Homestay.com offer various options for homestays in Ecuador.

3. Eco-Lodges: If you're an eco-conscious traveler, Ecuador has numerous eco-lodges that blend sustainability with comfort. These lodges are often located in breathtaking natural settings, providing a unique opportunity to connect with nature while minimizing your environmental impact. Some notable eco-lodges include Mashpi Lodge in the cloud forest and Napo Wildlife Center in the Amazon rainforest.

Things to Do:

1. Explore Quito's Historic Center: Begin your solo adventure in Quito by exploring its UNESCO World Heritage-listed historic center. Wander through its cobblestone streets, visit iconic landmarks such as the Basilica del Voto Nacional and Plaza Grande, and immerse yourself in the city's vibrant atmosphere.

2. Hike the Quilotoa Loop: For outdoor enthusiasts, the Quilotoa Loop is a must-do. This multi-day trek takes you through picturesque Andean villages, stunning landscapes, and culminates at the breathtaking Quilotoa Crater Lake. Along the way, interact with friendly locals, savor traditional cuisine, and enjoy the serenity of the Andean highlands.

3. Explore the Galapagos Islands: No visit to Ecuador is complete without experiencing the unique wildlife and landscapes of the Galapagos Islands. Join a guided tour or opt for a solo adventure by hopping on inter-island ferries. Snorkel with sea lions, observe giant tortoises, and marvel at the incredible biodiversity that inspired Charles Darwin's theory of evolution.

Staying Safe:

1. Research and Plan Ahead: Before embarking on your solo journey, research the areas you plan to visit and familiarize yourself with local customs and safety precautions. Be aware of any travel advisories and consult reliable sources such as government websites or travel forums for up-to-date information.

2. Blend In: While exploring Ecuador, it's advisable to dress modestly and avoid flashy jewelry or expensive gadgets. By blending in with the locals, you reduce the chances of becoming a target for theft or scams.

3. Stay Connected: Ensure you have a reliable means of communication, such as a local SIM card or portable Wi-Fi device. This will allow you to stay connected with loved ones and easily access emergency services if needed.

4. Trust Your Instincts: While Ecuador is generally a safe country, it's important to trust your instincts and be cautious, especially when venturing out at night or in unfamiliar areas. Avoid isolated places and always inform someone about your whereabouts.

Conclusion:

Traveling solo in Ecuador offers endless opportunities for adventure, cultural immersion, and self-discovery. By following these tips and exercising caution, you can make the most of your solo journey, create unforgettable memories, and return home with a newfound appreciation for this beautiful country and its people.

Chapter 42: Tips for Traveling on a Budget in Ecuador

Introduction:

Traveling to Ecuador on a budget can be an incredible experience, allowing you to explore the country's natural wonders, vibrant culture, and rich history without breaking the bank. In this chapter, we will provide you with valuable tips on where to stay, things to do, and how to save money during your adventure in Ecuador.

1. Affordable Accommodation Options:

a) Hostels: Ecuador offers a wide range of budget-friendly hostels throughout the country. These establishments provide comfortable and affordable accommodation, often with communal areas where you can meet fellow travelers.

b) Guesthouses: Look for guesthouses or family-run accommodations, which can offer a more authentic experience while being easier on your wallet.

c) Homestays: Consider staying with a local family through homestay programs. This not only provides an affordable lodging option but also allows you to immerse yourself in Ecuadorian culture.

2. Dining on a Budget:

a) Local Eateries: Opt for local restaurants and street food stalls to enjoy traditional Ecuadorian cuisine at a fraction of the cost compared to tourist-oriented establishments.

b) Markets: Explore local markets where you can find fresh produce, snacks, and affordable meals. This is an excellent opportunity to sample local delicacies while saving money.

c) Self-catering: If your accommodation allows, take advantage of the kitchen facilities to prepare your own meals. This can significantly cut down your food expenses.

3. Transportation:

a) Public Transportation: Utilize Ecuador's extensive public transportation network, including buses and trains, which are not only affordable but also offer a chance to interact with locals.

b) Shared Taxis: When traveling short distances within cities, consider sharing a taxi with other passengers to split the fare.

c) Hitchhiking: While hitchhiking is not for everyone, it can be a viable option for adventurous travelers looking to save money on transportation costs. Exercise caution and use your judgment when hitchhiking.

4. Free and Low-Cost Activities:

a) Explore Nature: Ecuador is renowned for its breathtaking landscapes and national parks. Take advantage of the country's natural beauty by hiking, camping, or simply enjoying the scenery, all of which are low-cost or free activities.

b) Cultural Experiences: Immerse yourself in Ecuadorian culture by attending local festivals, visiting museums during free admission days, or exploring vibrant markets.

c) Volunteer Opportunities: Consider volunteering with local organizations or eco-projects. This not only allows you to give back but also provides opportunities to connect with the community and experience Ecuador from a unique perspective.

5. Money-Saving Tips:

a) Bargain: Don't hesitate to negotiate prices, especially in local markets or when purchasing souvenirs.

b) Research and Plan: Take the time to research and plan your itinerary in advance. This will help you identify budget-friendly options and avoid unnecessary expenses.

c) Travel Off-Season: Consider traveling during the shoulder seasons when prices for accommodation and flights are generally lower.

Conclusion:

Traveling on a budget in Ecuador is not only possible but also a fantastic way to experience the country's beauty and culture. By following the tips provided in this chapter, you can make the most of your trip while keeping your expenses under control. Remember, Ecuador offers a wealth of affordable accommodation, delicious local cuisine, and countless free or low-cost activities, ensuring an unforgettable journey without breaking the bank.

Chapter 43: Tips for Traveling Responsibly in Ecuador

Introduction:

Ecuador, a country known for its incredible biodiversity and rich cultural heritage, offers travelers a unique experience. However, it is important to travel responsibly to minimize your impact on the environment and culture. In this chapter, we will provide you with valuable tips on how to make your journey through Ecuador an ethical and sustainable one.

1. Respect the Environment:

Ecuador's natural wonders, such as the Galapagos Islands, the Amazon Rainforest, and the Andes Mountains, are delicate ecosystems that require protection. As a responsible traveler, follow these guidelines:

a. Stay on designated trails to avoid damaging fragile flora and fauna.

b. Dispose of waste properly, using designated bins or taking it with you.

c. Conserve water and energy by taking shorter showers and turning off lights when not in use.

d. Choose eco-friendly accommodations that implement sustainable practices.

2. Support Local Communities:

Ecuador boasts a diverse cultural heritage, and engaging with local communities can enhance your travel experience while supporting their economic growth. Consider the following:

a. Stay in community-run lodges or homestays, which contribute directly to local economies.

b. Buy locally produced handicrafts and souvenirs, ensuring your money goes directly to artisans and their families.

c. Respect local customs and traditions, seeking permission before taking photographs of individuals or sacred sites.

d. Opt for local guides who possess extensive knowledge of the region's history, culture, and environment.

3. Minimize Plastic Waste:

Plastic pollution is a global concern, and Ecuador is no exception. Take steps to reduce your plastic footprint:

a. Carry a reusable water bottle and refill it at designated water stations or use water purification tablets.

b. Bring a reusable shopping bag to avoid using plastic bags when purchasing groceries or souvenirs.

c. Refuse single-use plastic items such as straws, cutlery, and plastic-wrapped products.

d. Participate in beach clean-ups or community initiatives aimed at reducing plastic waste.

4. Conserve Wildlife:

Ecuador is home to an astonishing array of wildlife, including rare and endangered species. To ensure their protection:

a. Adhere to designated wildlife viewing guidelines and maintain a safe distance from animals.

b. Avoid purchasing products made from endangered species, such as ivory or turtle shells.

c. Choose responsible tour operators who prioritize animal welfare and conservation efforts.

d. Educate yourself about local wildlife and ecosystems, fostering a deeper understanding and appreciation for their importance.

Conclusion:

By implementing these responsible travel tips, you can explore the wonders of Ecuador while minimizing your impact on the environment and culture. Remember, each decision you make as a traveler has the power to create positive change. Embrace the beauty of

Ecuador with a mindful and sustainable approach, leaving behind only footprints and taking home memories that will last a lifetime.

Printed by Libri Plureos GmbH in Hamburg, Germany